I've given my life to building bridges in the name of Jesus. *Dancing in No Man's Land* will become a valuable tool for those laboring with me. If you care about reconciliation, truth, and peace, this book is for you. Brian Jennings digs underneath the layers of hostility in our world and shows us how to emerge in the light. Our families, communities, and country will be radically changed when we begin living the principles from this book. I pray the change will begin with you.

> **DR. JOHN M. PERKINS**, cofounder of Christian Community Development Association (CCDA); founder and president emeritus of the John & Vera Mae Perkins Foundation; cofounder of Christian Community Health Fellowship (CCHF); author of *Let Justice Roll Down*

I have a friend with great courage. Rather than choosing to battle and scheme from the protection of a fortified bunker, Brian Jennings has elected to venture out and offer peace. Do you long to offer hope to those outside your hunkered-down beliefs? Well, *Dancing in No Man's Land* will equip and enable you to leave your bunker and engage with others in peaceful dialogue. There is a land between the bunkers that only a few find. Brian Jennings will show you the way.

> **KYLE IDLEMAN**, pastor; author of *Not a Fan* and *Grace Is Greater*

In these times, when it seems like we're surrounded by conversations waiting to go wrong, I'm grateful for Brian's call back to the way of Jesus. Let's step forward into our relationships with thoughtfulness and wisdom, understanding that truth and grace work best when offered together.

> **AUBREY SAMPSON**, speaker; church planter; author of *Overcomer: Breaking Down the Walls of Shame and Rebuilding Your Soul*

In his Sermon on the Mount, Jesus calls us to be "peacemakers," not "peacekeepers." There's an important and profound difference between those two. Peacekeepers hunker down in the bunker, prepared to deal with any conflict that may stumble upon them, but peacemakers get out of the bunker, venture into no man's land, and do the hard work of "making" peace. In this well-written, engaging, and practical book,

Brian Jennings doesn't just provide the motivation to get out of our bunkers and point toward a safe path through no man's land—he also reveals the steps necessary to ultimately dance in the midst of our journey toward a more peaceful world.

> **ARRON CHAMBERS**, pastor; author of *Eats with Sinners: Loving like Jesus* and *Devoted*

Brian writes with clarity, passion, and simplicity about issues that are critical to anyone who longs to find a faithful way to engage in a divisive culture. His engagement with Scripture as well as culturally significant moments makes this a helpful and challenging read. His pastoral passion is clear and compelling throughout the work—a strong, constructive read!

> **CASEY TYGRETT**, author of *Becoming Curious: A Spiritual Practice of Asking Questions*

For anyone wanting discipleship toward truth and peace, Jennings offers a desperately needed guide to recognize the idols of "bunker living" and learn to leave them behind. Of course, entering no man's land won't be easy or painless. But, beloved church, please listen to this trustworthy guide. Let's navigate the complications of this age with Jesus' own prayer in sight: unity.

> **CATHERINE MCNIEL**, author of *Long Days of Small Things: Motherhood as a Spiritual Discipline*

Bunkers feel safe and comfortable. In a complex world, living in a bunker seems reasonable. Brian Jennings, however, reveals to us how our bunkers, silos, and self-segregation away from those who think and live differently from us are actually a form of war rather than peacemaking. When we think we're being protective, we are actually being aggressive in ways that distract from the gospel of Jesus. But more than that, Brian shows us paths to peace and freedom.

> **SEAN PALMER**, author of *Unarmed Empire: In Search of Beloved Community*; teaching pastor at Ecclesia Houston; cohost of *Not So Black and White* (podcast)

DANCING IN NO MAN'S LAND

DANCING IN
NO MAN'S LAND

MOVING WITH PEACE AND TRUTH
IN A HOSTILE WORLD

BRIAN JENNINGS

NavPress

A NavPress resource published in alliance
with Tyndale House Publishers, Inc.

NAVPRESS®

NavPress is the publishing ministry of The Navigators, an international Christian organization and leader in personal spiritual development. NavPress is committed to helping people grow spiritually and enjoy lives of meaning and hope through personal and group resources that are biblically rooted, culturally relevant, and highly practical.

For more information, visit www.NavPress.com.

Dancing in No Man's Land: Moving with Peace and Truth in a Hostile World

Copyright © 2018 by Brian Jennings. All rights reserved.

A NavPress resource published in alliance with Tyndale House Publishers, Inc.

NAVPRESS and the NAVPRESS logo are registered trademarks of NavPress, The Navigators, Colorado Springs, CO. *TYNDALE* is a registered trademark of Tyndale House Publishers, Inc. Absence of ® in connection with marks of NavPress or other parties does not indicate an absence of registration of those marks.

The Team:
Don Pape, Publisher
Caitlyn Carlson, Acquisitions Editor
Elizabeth Symm, Copy Editor
Julie Chen, Designer

Interior photograph of coin copyright © by Gunthram/Wikimedia Commons. All rights reserved.

Interior illustration of hourglass copyright © by Pixel Bazaar/Creative Market. All rights reserved.

Cover photograph of clouds copyright © by John Hult/Unsplash.com. All rights reserved.

Cover photograph of WWI destruction taken by Ernest Brooks/Imperial War Museum.

Cover illustration of red cloth copyright © by Natis/Adobe Stock. All rights reserved.

Published in association with the literary agent Don Gates of The Gates Group, www.the-gates-group.com.

All Scripture quotations, unless otherwise indicated, are taken from the Holy Bible, *New International Version,*® *NIV.*® Copyright © 1973, 1978, 1984, 2011 by Biblica, Inc.® Used by permission. All rights reserved worldwide. Scripture quotations marked ESV are taken from *The Holy Bible*, English Standard Version® (ESV®), copyright © 2001 by Crossway, a publishing ministry of Good News Publishers. Used by permission. All rights reserved. Scripture quotations marked MSG are taken from *THE MESSAGE*, copyright © 1993, 1994, 1995, 1996, 2000, 2001, 2002 by Eugene H. Peterson. Used by permission of NavPress. All rights reserved. Represented by Tyndale House Publishers, Inc. Scripture quotations marked NLV are taken from the HOLY BIBLE, New Life Version. Copyright © 1969–2003 by Christian Literature International, P. O. Box 777, Canby, OR 97013. Used by permission. Scripture quotations marked AMP are taken from the Amplified Bible,® copyright © 2015 by The Lockman Foundation. Used by permission. www.Lockman.org.

Some of the anecdotal illustrations in this book are true to life and are included with the permission of the persons involved. All other illustrations are composites of real situations, and any resemblance to people living or dead is purely coincidental.

For information about special discounts for bulk purchases, please contact Tyndale House Publishers at csresponse@tyndale.com, or call 1-800-323-9400.

Cataloging-in-Publication Data is available.

ISBN 978-1-63146-773-8

Printed in the United States of America

24	23	22	21	20	19	18
7	6	5	4	3	2	1

Beth,

as the Lord sent a raven to Elijah,

he sent you to me.

CONTENTS

ACKNOWLEDGMENTS

Cole, Levi, Shurabe, and Hope: I love you with every breath. I'm so proud of you.

Highland Park Christian Church: Thank you for encouraging me to write and for selflessly loving my family. José, Matt, and Michelle, maybe the next book should include all those quotes Dave gets away with in staff meetings.

Mom and Dad: You instilled in me the commitment to do what is right and the heart to care for people.

Raynisha, Rachel, and David: Our home misses you. Our bunk bed is still here.

Kenneth Stewart: I'm forever thankful for our friendship.

Sarah Booe: You were the absolute perfect person to help me launch this project. Thanks for giving your immense skills and great care.

Sean Palmer and Caleb Kaltenbach: I read every book you recommended, and your encouragement carried me far.

Lance Schaubert: You did more than improve the writing; you improved the writer.

Don Gates: Thanks for believing in me and taking the great effort to represent my work.

Caitlyn and NavPress: A writer can't ask for more than to have a publisher pulling for their project and making it better all along the way.

Heavenly Father: Few things have so clearly been given to me by you. I'm not sure why you entrusted this idea to me, but I pray I've been a good steward. It's a joy to follow you.

Many embarked upon a quest to find the light

by digging deeper in the dirt.

But a few tried climbing toward the sun.

INTRODUCTION

Whoever loves a quarrel loves sin; whoever builds a high gate invites destruction.

PROVERBS 17:19

IT WAS THE FALL OF 1914.

This war was different from those that had come before. The invention of the machine gun, as well as other high-powered weapons, meant that armies could no longer charge their foes without suffering mass casualties. And so, as Allied forces beat back the German army, the Germans dug in, literally. The earth protected them, allowing them to hold their ground.

The Allied forces realized they couldn't advance, so they dug in too.

What began with small foxholes, bunkers, and ditches developed into thirty-five thousand miles of trenches that crisscrossed war-torn Europe. Offering protection from enemy fire, these trenches stalemated many battles, sometimes for years. The longer the armies stayed, the deeper, longer, and more secure their entrenchments grew.

Knowing the enemy bunker lay as close as fifty yards away, soldiers learned to lie low in the trench. Leaving their bunker or peeking over the top could well be their last move. Barbed wire stretched across the tops of bunkers and through the land between—no man's land. Snipers found vantage points from which they could shoot at soldiers daring to move out of their hole. Advancement was almost impossible.

Bunkers grew in sophistication, but most of their conditions were detestable. Some soldiers drowned in the mud. Some died of disease. Some lost feet due to trench foot. Many died from bullets, shells, or poison gas. All suffered from trying to figure out what to do with sewage, dead bodies, flies, and rats.

Still, if you were in World War I, hunkering down in a bunker, trench, or foxhole might give you the best chance of survival. You could lob grenades and stick your gun over the top while keeping your head low. The problem is that if someone with a better view wasn't giving you an idea of what was going on, you couldn't leave your bunker until the other side either surrendered or died. Even then, you may have felt safer staying right where you were.

With each side holed up, refusing to talk and engaging only through violence, the bunkers of war were void of peacemaking. The bunkers of life are no different.

Has a disagreement with a friend escalated to the point where you now treat them as a foe? Have you been in a conversation where no one is listening? Have you watched family members choose sides in a feud? Are you in a war of differing opinions, with wounds on all sides and no hope in sight?

Or perhaps a political ideology has lured you into lining up dissenters in your crosshairs. When a news story breaks, you immediately declare an alliance and an enemy. Do you only listen to those who agree with you and arm you for battle? Are you tired of shooting and being shot during every election?

In our culture, we hunker down in our opinions and beliefs, poking our heads up only to lob angry words at the opposing side. If someone disagrees with us on an issue, we are quick to label them "enemy," lash out, and attack. We launch our assault from a bunker filled with like-minded thinkers. Advancement is almost impossible. And we can't know what is actually going on because our heads are below the dirt.

We see people fighting from their bunkers, hiding in their bunkers. Sometimes we even see people leaving their bunkers only to join another, turning their weapons on their former allies.

Oh, and if you dare to leave your bunker to talk to the other side, you'll get shot from both sides.

This mind-set is killing us. It's killing friendships and families.

Killing civility and discourse. Killing businesses and organizations. Killing churches and charities. Killing respect and influence.

There has to be another way. A better way. A land beyond the bunkers.

One of the great challenges of our day is to learn how to pursue truth and peace—at the same time. Somehow, Jesus did it, as have a few others. But it's not our normal. We feel an incessant pressure to choose either truth or peace, as if the two can't be trusted to sit next to each other without drawing blood.

Neither truth nor peace can create wholeness without the other. A husband's complaints against his wife may be true. A wife's complaints against her husband may be true. If they only care about these truths without also seeking peace, their relationship is doomed. Truth won't even matter anymore. It becomes distorted, manipulated, and angry from a bunker.

But simply pursuing peace, setting truth aside, is its own kind of bunker. Devaluing truth never leads to actual peace. It only causes chaos. Those who demand complete tolerance (accepting every opinion from every person) seem to only be tolerant of those with whom they agree. They label their enemies as "intolerant." But to be intolerant of intolerant people is itself . . . intolerant.

And then there are times, when a controversial topic makes headlines, that many of us kick both truth and peace to the curb. Neither of those, after all, serves our agenda when we're angry. But rejecting them altogether is the worst thing we can do.

To find the better way, we must seek truth, and we must also seek peace. We must seek them both at the same time.

If we cannot learn to live in truth away from the bunkers, if we cannot learn to set aside our need to be right and learn to love others even when we disagree—how will our families, schools, businesses, neighborhoods, and churches heal? What will become of our world? Who will make peace? Who will bring clarity? Who will take the risk? Who will change the world?

If you long for things to be different, I pray God will graciously use the words on these pages to encourage you: You are not alone. People all over this planet share your longings for a different way, a different world. The hostility they see all around sickens them. They long for healing and wholeness. But our longings won't bloom into reality without radically altered hearts, minds, and souls.

I'm asking you to reject the notion that the path of truth forks away from the path of peace. Refuse to be enticed away from either. There's a land between the bunkers. Only a few find it. They've been misunderstood and accused of everything under the sun. People in the bunkers hated them when they left. The wanderers of the less-traveled land die every day, yet if you catch a glimpse of them beyond the barbed wire and smoke, you'll see the most peculiar thing—they are dancing. In that place where truth and peace dwell, there is joy. You can dance too in that frightful, wonderful land between, that place called no man's land.

In this book, we're going to take a journey together into dangerous healing, out of our bunkers and into no man's land. Has hostility seeped into your own life? Have you chosen sides? Identifying your true coordinates will prepare you to map out a new route. World change starts with self-examination.

Part 2 aims to inspire and equip you to choose a new way. You'll stuff your gear bag with timeless principles and stories of hope. You'll learn from those who changed their world, avoiding bunkers at every turn. Clear minds and gentle words really do prevail.

In part 3, we'll lock arms, climb, crawl, and change. I'll share how I'm trying to live in no man's land and offer you hope for navigating some of life's most volatile issues.

While the principles in this book can be applied by anyone, our hope rests in the Lord. History reveals that mere human efforts fall apart in the end. I pray God's hand will act in you and through you more magnificently than is humanly possible.

Be warned, the struggle for peacemaking and clear thinking is hard, grueling work. Mud may swallow your ankles with every step. Some will misunderstand you. Others will line you up in their crosshairs.

Thankfully, you have the examples of brave men and women to

follow, and you have the opportunity to learn from the source of all wisdom. Lean into this. Equip yourself to be a gentle and clear voice of healing in your world.

We need you to do this.

For the love of God, get out of your bunker.

PART I

BUNKEROLOGY

If there's just one kind of folks, why can't they get along with each other? If they're all alike, why do they go out of their way to despise each other?

HARPER LEE, *To Kill a Mockingbird*

CHAPTER 1

ROOTS

Why We Step into Bunkers

Bunker mentality: An attitude of extreme defensiveness and self-justification based on an often exaggerated sense of being under persistent attack from others.[1]

FEW THINGS MAKE ME HAPPIER than a cup of coffee and free parking on a cold day in downtown Chicago. That's why I am so familiar with Division Street, where you can find a shopping center that has both. (I'd tell you where, but I can't have you taking my secret spot.)

For the past eleven years I've led a Chicago trip for high-school students, where they learn from and work alongside two of my favorite ministries in the world: First Christian Church and By The Hand Club for Kids.[2] I've also traveled to Chicago to play, see friends, and attend meetings. There's a lot to love about the city—a lot of beauty. But there is a lot that should concern us too.

When Chicago announced mass school closings in 2013, Manierre Elementary families worried. The plan called for Manierre students to attend Jenner Elementary. It's only a short walk, but the change required them to cross Division Street. Manierre kids aren't supposed to cross Division. That's the rule on the street, and gangs enforce it.[3]

One of our partner ministries buses or walks children home, taking the appropriate routes to ensure their safety. The gang members seldom care if a kid is involved in a rival gang or not. They just know someone's walking across the street from a neighborhood that plays host to rival gangs. Animosity runs deep, spanning generations. Sadly, this is reality for many children.

What lies at the root of the bunkers we dig into? While we may not face the stark division between gangs, we all face division in our everyday lives. At work, when we're asked to side with a coworker or a boss. In politics, when our choice of candidate supposedly defines so much about who we are. In relationships, when longstanding wounds flare up and people decide who they most believe.

Bunkers emerge in many ways, but there are three common roots: fear, pride, and the cycle of anger.

Fear pushes us deeper into our bunkers and keeps us there, telling us that no good will come of not holding our ground. On Division Street, fear isolates neighbors who only live a block apart. Isolation feeds their paranoia. Any outsider is an imminent threat.

Fear's close cousin is pride—the belief that we know more and better and therefore have the right to our bunker. Pride keeps us in our bunker because we can't imagine a good reason to leave. Division Street won't see peace until people are willing to swallow their pride. Humility can feel as if we're betraying the people in our bunker and the people we once were (or currently are).

As pride and fear work together, we become more entrenched, and our feuds escalate into an unending cycle. Some people are your enemies just because that's how it's always been. You could find some rivals on Division Street who'd say the same thing you'd hear from a family member: "I don't even know what we were arguing about." It's important that we understand the roots of the bunker mentality before we do anything else, because only by yanking out the roots will we be able to move forward in healthy and productive ways.

On Division Street, gang members have drawn lines. They've tied their loyalty to those in their gang. They aren't interested in open-minded dialogue but are instead obsessed with power and protection. They personify bunker dwellers.

But if we let fear, pride, and anger control us, so do we.

FEAR

Fear can paralyze.

I discovered this years ago, when I went with a group of friends to play paintball. The owner of the place was a skinny, scraggly-haired guy who looked like Shaggy from the old Scooby-Doo cartoons. "Shaggy" explained the game to us, delighting in telling us all the ways we could be injured. Then he let us shoot some practice rounds.

The speed of the small paint-filled balls both excited and terrified us. We realized this game was going to hurt a lot worse than a simple game of tag. One of my friends, who wore a mesh tank top that day, decided to stop teasing me for wearing so many layers.

The owner divided us into teams, sent us to opposite sides, and told us our objective: to shoot everyone on the other team. When he yelled "Go!" all cocky banter subsided. Each team wanted to win, but we also wanted to avoid pain.

When I found myself pinned down by enemy fire, paintballs whizzing by my head, I was afraid to move from my little ditch behind a tree. But surrendering seemed too unmanly. I finally worked up the nerve to leap out for a brave assault.

Agony quickly replaced my bravado. I was left with multiple welts as reminders of my foolishness.

Even in a silly game like paintball, we can be overpowered by fear. And in life, we find ourselves facing many things a lot more painful— and a lot more fear-inducing—than paintballs.

Fear can paralyze, keeping us from moving forward. A friend of mine told me she could never give her heart away. She wanted a happy marriage, but past pain crippled her willingness to be vulnerable. She spent her childhood trying to fix her bleeding heart. Memories of abandonment, neglect, and abuse haunted her. Eventually, instead of trying to fix her heart, she attempted to protect it by never giving it away.

When we're overcome with fear, bunkers feel safe. We're afraid engaging will make things worse. We can't handle feeling so vulnerable. Fear pushes us to dig in deeper, to hide away, to avoid the scary space outside our bunker.

To be fair, our fear is not without merit. Have you ever felt defeated after trying to bring peace to a warring marriage? Have you ever noticed what a rarity it is for someone to change their political views? Opinions abound, but why does the shouting leave minds unchanged? Fear exhausts us, drains our motivation, and pins us down. Only once we recognize how fear is controlling us can we have any hope of moving out of our bunker.

In the case of my hurting friend, fear drove out love. Our hearts only have room for one or the other. If it's true that "there is no fear in love. But perfect love drives out fear" (1 John 4:18), we can also assume that fear can cast out love. Are your roots growing in fear or love?

PRIDE

In many ways, pride addresses what fear causes. Fear makes us feel out of control and powerless. Pride tricks us into believing we have control and all the power. Pride keeps us in our bunker just as much as fear does, keeping us right where we are out of the belief that no one else is as right as we are.

When the great King Solomon died, his son Rehoboam was handed the crown. The people begged him to lighten the oppressive, crushing workload forced upon them by his father.[4]

King Rehoboam told them he would consider their request and give them an answer in three days. A group of wise, experienced advisers said, "If you will be kind to these people and please them and give them a favorable answer, they will always be your servants" (2 Chronicles 10:7). But his group of foolish buddies advised, "Now tell them, 'My little finger is thicker than my father's waist. My father laid on you a heavy yoke; I will make it even heavier. My father scourged you with whips; I will scourge you with scorpions'" (2 Chronicles 10:10-11).

Rehoboam's pride clouded his judgment. He listened to his foolish friends, choosing to rule as a tyrant bully. He was the king, thinking he deserved to do whatever he wanted.

The Israelites felt completely abandoned. The country was no longer their country. As for Rehoboam, his life was soon in peril. He escaped the self-inflicted rebellion, but his Chief of Forced Labor was not so lucky. (You know you're a bad leader when you have a Chief of Forced Labor.) The people stoned that man to death. He was simply the ugly face of the king's pride—pride that led to his demise and, in some ways, the demise of the nation.

Romans 12:16 says, "Live in harmony with one another. Do not be haughty, but associate with the lowly. Never be wise in your own sight" (ESV). Hebrews 7:26 uses a variation of the word translated "haughty" to describe Jesus' exaltation above the heavens. The word aptly describes him but ought never to describe us. A haughty person acts as if they deserve the exaltation. They assume they are high above the rest.

Haughty people love their bunkers so much that they can't possibly imagine ever being wrong. The progression may go like this:

1. I think I am right.
2. I know I am right.
3. Because I am right, they are wrong.
4. Because I must stand for what's right, I must attack those who are wrong.
5. Because I am right, I'm better than them.

You may get to step 1 (thinking you are right) quickly, and there's nothing wrong with that. You can even have a civil and productive discussion at step 3 (believing you are right and the other is wrong). But step 4 (attacking the person with whom you disagree) drops you straight into a bunker. It's why you need great discernment about ever moving past step 1.

Sometimes you'll need to drop all opinions and just learn. Other times, you should hold a loose opinion or strong conviction. It depends on the subject. You can do all of those things well in the first three steps.

But once you move to step 4 or 5, you harm the relationship. It's rare for a person to work their way out of their bunker and back up the progression. Once you are right and better than me, and once I'm wounded from your attacks, our relationship plummets into deep trouble. Pride will hamper any honest attempts toward truth or peace.

DEFENSE TO OFFENSE

Fear and pride work in a destructive cycle, making us defensive of our position, closed to considering any ideas from opposing bunkers. And in our defensiveness, we end up navigating serious life issues as if we were rooting for college football teams.

When I moved to Tulsa, Oklahoma, in 1998, I quickly learned that Tulsa is made up of three types of people: Oklahoma Sooner fans, Oklahoma State Cowboy fans, and people who are sick of hearing about both of them. (Few fall into this third category.)

People here are crazy about college sports, especially college football. And while there's some good-natured ribbing, there's some genuine hatred, too. Both colleges have had their fair share of scandals, dishonest coaches, and law-breaking players. Every time a distasteful story hits the news, some fans of the other school act as though Santa has landed on the roof. They laugh and mock. They grow giddy with excitement. But the truth is, they don't need scandals and other failures to propel the hostility forward. The simple division of sports loyalties can create an unhealthy anger and foster dehumanization of the other side.

Unfortunately, we can increasingly see this scenario playing out in a host of other contexts. I once officiated a wedding in which I was warned about how much the two families disliked each other. The ushers were told to be careful to seat people on their designated sides of the chapel. I asked the groom why the two families had such animosity. He couldn't remember. It wasn't anything big. A small disagreement had spiraled out of control.

Proverbs 18:19 says, "A brother wronged is more unyielding than a fortified city; disputes are like the barred gates of a citadel." From boardrooms to living rooms, this verse is played out right in front of us every day. As we recoil from fear and cling to our pride, our words become reactionary and careless. One harsh word can spiral us into a never-ending feud:

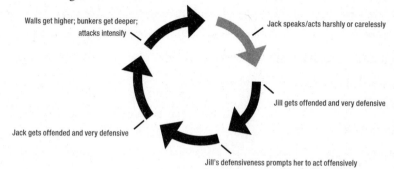

Walls get higher; bunkers get deeper; attacks intensify

Jack speaks/acts harshly or carelessly

Jill gets offended and very defensive

Jill's defensiveness prompts her to act offensively

Jack gets offended and very defensive

When feuds escalate, the roots of our bunker mentality grow into a poisonous tree, and everyone loses. Wounded people tend to wound people. Hurt people hurt people. The offended become the offenders. And when a war breaks out, people choose sides.

We're all too familiar with this in our culture. It's been happening for a while, but I found myself first really bowled over by it in 2012.

President Obama's signature piece of legislation during his first term in office was the Affordable Care Act (often called Obamacare). Debates about the government's role in health-care issues quickly escalated across the country. Heated arguments erupted everywhere: the halls of Congress, TV and radio talk shows, Internet blogs, and many personal conversations.

People clambered to their bunkers.

The health-care issue became dominated by two extreme camps. Some clambered to a bunker that accused, "If you support this bill, you hate our country." Others shot back from an opposing bunker, "If you do not support this bill, you hate the poor." People said these things in many different ways, but the message was clear: "You are either with me or against me."

Do you see how this language forced people into separate camps? There was no tolerance for those unwilling to declare an enemy, to pick sides. Pride and fear mingled, putting people into bunkers—pride in one's own position being absolutely right and fear of the implications of the other position—and the cycle of anger around health care continues even as I write this book years later. *Sigh.*

I'm not advocating we think unclearly or uncritically about important issues. Just the opposite. Health care and our government's role in such things deserve robust discussion and debate. I'm just suggesting we learn to do so without lobbing a grenade that will blast destruction in every direction. Extreme statements don't help anyone think clearly about an issue. They only divide people and cloud clarity.

If you find yourself in a bunker, mad and ready to attack, you need to ask God to examine your roots. You probably won't spot the problems on your own—few of us can. Each of us should turn our ears to wise people and the quiet whispers of God. Fear, pride, and violent cycles poison roots. The leaves on the plant may look green for a while, but not for long. The toxins in the roots will soon spread, and the whole plant will wither.

Tim Keller taught me to look for the "sin beneath the sin."[5] It's easy to notice when someone is arrested for abusing his wife, but we'll have to look closer to find what's really wrong. Beneath the eye-catching sin is a "sin beneath the sin" (like unresolved anger). It's this "sin beneath the sin" that poisons roots, and it's not something we can fix. Only God heals hearts. Only God heals roots. Only he has the power to dig deep enough to repair our spiritual brokenness. It's his specialty.

REFLECTION QUESTIONS

1. Is fear driving out love in your life? From where does this fear come?

2. How are you tempted to be prideful? What helps you overcome that pride?

3. What cycles of hate or violence do you see in your world?

4. Is there a "sin beneath the sin" in your life that needs to be addressed?

5. Whom can you ask to help you grow healthier roots?

CHAPTER 2

SPIRITUAL
THREAT

———

*This war will be a violent incentive to Futurism, for we believe there
is no beauty except in strife, and no masterpiece without aggressiveness.*
C. R. W. NEVINSON

A FEW CHRISTMASES AGO, the *New York Daily News* reported a story that
lacked any holiday cheer:[1]

> A South Carolina family nearly decked each other in the halls
> Monday when two women began decorating the Christmas
> tree while a third was at work, cops said.
>
> The women—aged 76, 61 and 24—started fighting around
> 10:30 p.m., police said.
>
> Two hours later the fight was still going strong.

Soon, a fourth relative joined the fray. Finally, the police intervened:

> "During the course of the verbal argument, all four family
> members admitted to pushing each other and getting in (each
> others') faces," the report by Spartanburg County Sheriffs read.

. . . "All four family members stressed that their emotions had gotten the better of them . . ." the report read.

Ummm, no kidding. Bunkers threaten the peace of your family. Bunkers, in fact, pose a grave threat to every aspect of your life.

Thankfully, the family feud did not lead to death. But that's not always the case when lines are drawn. Armies have clashed over land, oil, religion, and ethnic domination. And . . . buckets?

From the late Middle Ages until the Renaissance, northern Italy divided into factions who supported rival political powers, which further intensified their border disputes. According to legend, in 1325, a huge conflict erupted when soldiers from the town of Modena stole an oak bucket from the nearby rival town of Bologna.[2] The thieves mockingly displayed the bucket for all to see.

Outraged, the Bolognese army marched to Modena to recover their bucket and pride. When the Modenese refused their demand, the Bolognese declared war. This event became known as the War for the Oaken Bucket.

Bologna summoned a mighty army from the Guelph cities. Thirty thousand men-at-arms, two thousand knights, and Pope John XXII himself joined the cause of reclaiming the bucket.

The Modenese, by contrast, only gathered five thousand men-at-arms and two thousand knights.

The two armies clashed on the afternoon of November 15 at Zappolino. Despite being outnumbered nearly five to one, the Modenese managed to rout the Bolognese in just two hours of battle. The Modenese pursued the Bolognese all the way to the walls of Bologna, where they flaunted their victory before their humiliated enemy. A total of four thousand men died that day. All because of a bucket.[3]

Bunkers threaten your community, your church, your world. And while we can laugh at the absurdity of stories like these, let's not mince words: Our propensity toward attacking one another—no matter how ridiculous or serious the issue—is a sin. We don't often think of it in those terms; after all, we tend to highlight certain sins, while minimizing "silly" other ones. We too often downplay sins like pride, jealousy, and arguing. Do we think these "other sins" will not lead to destruction too? Do we think that God cares little about them? Our very disregard for the spiritual dangers of the bunkers around us poses a threat.

THE UGLY LIST

In Galatians chapter 5 we find a beautiful list of the characteristics of God, the characteristics his Spirit matures in us—better known as the fruit of the Spirit.[4] But there's another list preceding that one, and it lacks any sort of beauty. Paul instead speaks of terrible, ugly things, things that threaten our souls:

> The acts of the flesh are obvious: sexual immorality, impurity and debauchery; idolatry and witchcraft; *hatred, discord, jealousy, fits of rage, selfish ambition, dissensions, factions and envy*; drunkenness, orgies, and the like.
>
> GALATIANS 5:19-21, EMPHASIS MINE

Eight consecutive sins fall under the category of "not getting along." **Apparently, getting along is a *huge* deal to God.** These eight sins drive wedges into relationships, churches, and countries. They divide and fracture. Greek scholar Kenny Boles says the following about factions:[5]

> The Greek word for "choosing up sides" was *hairesis* (HI reh sis). In addition to its use in political situations it was often used in the context of choosing to join a particular school of philosophy. In this sense a *hairesis* was a "selection" or "choice." When Josephus chose which sect of the Jews he would join (the Essenes, the Sadducees, or the Pharisees), his "choice" was the "sect" (*hairesis*) of the Pharisees.
>
> It's natural to want to choose up sides—natural, but wrong. When Paul listed the works of the flesh ("acts of the sinful nature") in Galatians 5:19-21, he included the plural form of

the word *hairesis* ("factions," or choosing up sides). For those who are led by the Spirit in the community of Christ, there is no room for choosing up sides—forming sects around favorite leaders or pet doctrines.

By the time *hairesis* came into the English language a thousand years later it had come to mean "heresy," choosing the wrong doctrine. Folks who see the word in the KJV often misunderstand, thinking that the sinful act lies in choosing the wrong leader or the wrong doctrine. But the sin is in the very act of choosing. Carnal men choose up sides; Christians stand together.

Sometimes I'm the carnal human choosing up sides, as I did when two best friends got in an argument. If I'd tied Sharee and Rosalyn's shoelaces together, little would have changed, because they were always together. They were skipping through teenage life with joy and kindness, which is why the dispute between them caught me so off guard. As soon as I heard of their argument, I should have asked lots of questions. I should have tried to bring reconciliation. I should have paused.

Instead, I sinned. I immediately chose a side, which means I immediately chose an enemy.

I can still feel the turbulence in my soul when I chose. How could I have been so foolish? In my rush to declare a winner of their fight, I became a peacebreaker. I caused more separation between them.

When I realized my error, I began trying to undo the damage. God was gracious to me. The three of us reconciled, but it took a lot more pain and effort because of my stupidity. I felt fortunate to have emerged with peace. This story could have ended ugly.

Choosing sides seems so prevalent in today's culture, and, as in Paul's day, Christians are by no means immune. I've been guilty of pledging a peace-breaking, truth-sacrificing allegiance to disputing friends, political candidates, and religious schools of thought. I've mislabeled my idolatry as loyalty. We'll cover more of this ground later, but please examine your heart right now. Have you bunkered down with a political camp or religious circle and drawn a line of demarcation? Have you placed a political party, teacher, preacher, or leader on *the* throne?

Factions, fits of rage, jealousy, and the rest of the sins from the Galatians 5 list destroy community. They destroy us. That's why God includes these sins on the ugly list.

EXPELLED

The destruction of community should concern us deeply, because as the body of Christ, we are part of a community that is supposed to model Jesus Christ to the watching world. That's why we shouldn't be surprised by Paul's approach in Titus 3:1-2. For most of us, if we were leading an infant church, our first instinct would probably be to spread a positive message of hope. But in Paul's letter to his friend Titus, he hammers down on several threats to the church, including divisive church members. These people could cause great harm to the entire church, stripping the other believers of their potential. And hope vanishes in the midst of strife.

Paul doesn't pull any punches:

> Remind the people to be subject to rulers and authorities, to be obedient, to be ready to do whatever is good, to slander no one, to be peaceable and considerate, and always to be gentle toward everyone.

How different would the Internet be if we all committed to "slander no one," "be peaceable and considerate," and "always . . . be gentle toward everyone"? I increasingly hear about friends who have taken a weekend pause or even a prolonged fast from social media. Every single one of them told me how refreshing it was. It's not hard to figure out why—it's refreshing to reduce the amount of slander, arguments, and arrogance we allow into our souls. One prideful, rude comment can negate the impact of dozens of nice or neutral comments we read. Paul knew this, even two thousand years before the Internet came along.

How different would your life be if words like *peaceable*, *considerate*, and *gentle* dominated your family tree? How would your workplace be different? Your school? Your world?

> At one time we too were foolish, disobedient, deceived and
> enslaved by all kinds of passions and pleasures. We lived in
> malice and envy, being hated and hating one another.
>
> TITUS 3:3

Malice. Envy. Hating one another and being hated. Wow, that sounds like a miserable existence. The Bible honestly depicts this unsavory reality for so many people. But the Bible also shows us a different possibility. Did you notice that the above verse is in the past tense? Your current reality doesn't have to be your final destiny. Humans were created in a lush garden—what can be more peaceful than that? The Israelites were delivered from enslavement to the *Promised Land*. Jesus came as the *Prince of Peace*. The prophets tell of a day when a lion will lie down next to a lamb. The hope in Christ is that the malice and hate in this world don't have to have the final say in your life.

> This is a trustworthy saying. And I want you to stress these
> things, so that those who have trusted in God may be careful
> to devote themselves to doing what is good. These things
> are excellent and profitable for everyone. But avoid foolish
> controversies and genealogies and arguments and quarrels
> about the law, because these are unprofitable and useless.
>
> TITUS 3:8-9

As the gospel spread and more Jews committed to Christ, some argued over Old Testament (their written Scripture) interpretations in light of Jesus, who was the fulfillment of that Scripture. Some of those discussions needed to occur, but trivial arguments were clouding the important message while also stirring harsh words and hurt feelings.

We have to ask, "What were the concerns of Jesus?" Jesus said he came to seek and save the lost (Luke 19:10). When you are locked in a clear, Kingdom-minded vision, why would you ever engage in a foolish controversy?

One Sunday morning I overheard a lady arguing with our children's ministry volunteers about a new check-in policy. She thought it unnecessary and burdensome to take the extra moments to punch a name into a computer and wait for it to print out name tags. Everyone in the lobby knew exactly how she felt, including the guests standing behind her. I tried talking to them very loudly, hoping to drown out the rant.

Sometimes I'm the guilty party too. The moment I lose sight of God's mission, I'm capable of engaging in all sorts of stupid arguments and wasteful thoughts. One of the great blessings of following Christ is that he draws our minds, conversations, and actions into things that really matter, things he cares about.

> Warn a divisive person once, and then warn them a second
> time. After that, have nothing to do with them. You may
> be sure that such people are warped and sinful; they are
> self-condemned.
>
> TITUS 3:10-11

Do Paul's words seem overly harsh to you? His words apply to the church, but not those outside the church. The church has no business judging the world. We don't expect non–Christ followers to act as if they are following Christ.[6] However, God calls the church to lead holy lives—living in unity with one another.

Words like *cantankerous*, *feisty*, *argumentative*, *disagreeable*, and *bad-tempered* can describe a divisive person. Call it what you will, but God calls it *sin*. Divisiveness threatens all that the church is working toward, shoving both sides of an argument deep into bunkers and compromising the church's mission.

If the church disciplines someone, it's a regrettable last resort. The goal is to protect the church and her mission and to also convict the divisive person to repent.

NOT GOOD

I have an annoying habit of telling people "I'm good," even when I'm not. This happens a lot when I'm shopping. When the employee at the grocery store asks me if I need help, I say, "I'm good," even though I have no clue where to find the Indian spice my wife needs. Instead, I wander through the aisles so long that I soon forget what I was trying to find in the first place.

We see this same pride in a child attempting to pour milk on cereal, even though the gallon carton is disproportionately heavy. Sometimes we need to say, "Help me," instead of "I'm good."

My pride can hijack the time it takes me to complete a task or the quality of my attempts at a simple job, but it can do much worse. When I think "I'm good," I'm hindering the work God wants to do through me. It's only when I acknowledge my own frailty that I am useful.

When we look at the pride, the disunity, the anger, the bunkers around us, we might get discouraged or depressed. In Paul's letter to Titus, he doesn't leave him without hope:

> When the kindness and love of God our Savior appeared, he
> saved us, not because of righteous things we had done, but
> because of his mercy. He saved us through the washing of
> rebirth and renewal by the Holy Spirit, whom he poured out
> on us generously through Jesus Christ our Savior, so that,
> having been justified by his grace, we might become heirs
> having the hope of eternal life.
>
> TITUS 3:4-7

Your past does not write the script for your future. God's mercy is greater than your sins. You can be saved, not by your righteous deeds, but by God's goodness. Will you ask for help?

My friend Alice says she thinks it's usually easy for her to forgive others because she's forever amazed at how much God forgave her. That's the way it works. If you remember how much God has forgiven you, you'll be a humble person. You'll always know your great need for God, and he will erode your pride. Jesus said, "Whoever has been forgiven little loves little."[7] The truth is that we've been forgiven more than we can imagine.

Do you know what you get if you assemble a whole group of people who are convinced they are flawed and in need of God's grace and therefore are quick to forgive others? You get God's ideal for a family, church, community. You also get a group of people who will want to be around each other. Humility breeds unity.

Oftentimes, God gently prompts me to do something. But every once in a while, he thunders his intentions. Five years ago, as I opened my eyes to how often Christians were trampling people for the sake of a political point and how our entire culture seemed to throw gas at any divisive flame, I grew depressed about the bigger issues. I began to wonder with every cultural fight, "Who has the most to gain, and who has the most to lose?" I wasn't always sure about who had the most to gain. It seemed to be the media, politicians, and partisan groups, but I'm not sure. But I became convinced that usually it was the church who had the most to lose during these times. If the enemy could use an argument about health care, race, or the economy to split the church, he'd win and we'd lose—and no loss would be costlier for the entire planet. God has impressed this danger upon my heart, and I see warning signs every day. Staying out of the bunkers is a spiritual issue. The stakes are high for your soul and the people in your life. And, as we'll see in the next chapter, the impact of your choices will resonate further than you may have ever dreamed.

REFLECTION QUESTIONS

1. What's the most ridiculous fight you've ever seen?

2. Is there something silly (when placed in its proper perspective) that keeps causing you to fight?

3. Have you bunkered down with a personal preference, political camp, or religious circle and drawn an unnecessary line of demarcation?

4. Why is God so concerned about divisive people in the church?

5. When do you say to God, "I'm good," when you should be saying, "Help"?

CHAPTER 3

COLLATERAL DAMAGE

—————

The frontline soldier was only concerned with . . . a hundred yards or so on either side of him and that in front of him. We pinned sandbags to the side of the trench with cartridges to cover up corpses.
GEORGE COPPARD, ROYAL WEST SURREY REGIMENT, WWI

WHEN THE ALLIED AND German armies dug into bunkers in World War I, the new superior defenses began to outmatch offensive schemes. But not for long. Better defenses simply meant that scientists and soldiers needed to craft new offensives.

In an attempt to break the stalemate, the Germans introduced the world to poison gas. French soldiers were the first to die the slow, painful death delivered by gas. The Allies countered by issuing gas masks for their soldiers and attacking the Germans with their own poisonous concoctions.

The ugliness of war was in full bloom. Humans could now inhale death.

The thing about poison gas is that it's not very precise. It unintentionally kills the wounded soldier who poses no threat, the medic, the journalist, or the fleeing farmer. Today, we know of too many times innocent bystanders were killed by poison gas, bombs, or other large-scale weapons. We coldly refer to this as collateral damage.

Stray bullets don't slow down for the innocent. Victims find no comfort in learning that the shooter had someone else in their crosshairs.

Collateral damage isn't limited to the battlefield: It happens around us every day. When two managers battle for power within a company, they do not intend to hurt other employees . . . but the resulting tension, divisions, and factions impact anyone within striking distance. When a mom and dad quarrel, they do not intend to hurt their child . . . but the child internalizes the pain, tries to fix it, or hides away in fear.

And so it is in our world of bunkers. When people fight, a poison gas fills the air. Our anger and division spread to the people around us, leading to pain, devastation, and even a slow death.

UNINTENDED CONSEQUENCES

Divisiveness can ooze harm in all directions, even to future generations. If your parents chose a favorite child, you'll sympathize with Esau and Jacob.[1] They were twins, but not the kind who looked alike and spent all their time together. Esau was born a few seconds before Jacob. Because their culture honored the firstborn, Esau stood to receive more in life from his parents. This was fine with Isaac, their father. He preferred the rough and tough Esau. But Rebekah, their mother, preferred the quieter Jacob. Can you smell the trouble brewing?

As the boys grew into men, Rebekah persuaded Jacob to trick his brother and dad. The scheme worked, and Jacob scored what rightfully belonged to Esau: a special blessing. Esau was so enraged that he wanted to kill Jacob. Rebekah told Jacob to run for his life. He did, staying away from his brother for more than two decades.

The story of Jacob may sound familiar, but the story of his sons is so popular that it's been portrayed in books, in movies, and even on Broadway stages. Jacob had twelve sons. The second youngest was named Joseph, and the Bible tells us Jacob loved him more than any of the others.[2] He even made Joseph a coat nicer than anything his brothers had ever seen or worn (it was so colorful that some might describe it as "technicolor"). He committed the same parenting sin his father committed against him.

Joseph lacked the common sense to keep quiet about his dreams, which told of his brothers bowing to him. Resentment boiled in the older brothers until one day it spewed into a hideous plot. Away from their father's sight, they snatched Joseph, thought about leaving him in a well to die, but decided to sell him into slavery. They told Jacob that wild animals must've killed Joseph, leaving their father a broken man.

How much do you have to hate someone to sell them into slavery? How could a family be so broken? We can never excuse the behavior of the brothers, but we can draw a straight line back to their grandparents. Collateral damage seeped down the family tree.

When Isaac favored Esau and Rebekah hatched her scheme, they could've never imagined what they'd done to their grandchild Joseph. When you and I raise weapons from a bunker, we have no idea how far the poison gas will spread. Now that we know this, we should stop excusing it as *unintentional*.

THE WOUNDED

When we live in a bunker, we harm others. Some of the harmed we know, but some we'll never meet. Let's consider a few of the people most harmed, beginning with those for whom I'm most concerned.

// CHILDREN

Our family spends some hot summer days in a neighborhood swimming pool. One day, while making the feet-scorching journey from the kiddie pool to the big pool, my daughter and I caught a whiff of chlorine, sunblock, and drama.

Many lifeguards have six-pack abs. This one looked as if he were trying to hide a six-pack of beer under his shirt. We saw him using his voice and weight to run a few junior high kids out of the pool. As he turned away, he mumbled to another lifeguard, "I don't have anything against colored boys, but I'm not putting up with them acting like colored boys."

I would've been less horrified if an octopus had surfaced in the deep end.

Later, as we gathered our things to leave, I overheard the lifeguard's little brother tell his friends, "My brother kicked those stupid colored boys out of the pool." His insensitive words don't make him a bad, mean kid. They make him a normal kid, because normal kids repeat what they hear from their families.

Sadness splashed my heart. This boy, without rescue, will live in ignorance and soak others with prejudice.

Bunker living impacts the most innocent among us in profound ways. Bluntly, bunker living causes children to sin. It teaches them that it's okay to be ruthless, disrespectful, and foolish. It teaches them to think in a bubble. It teaches them that their bunker is the source of truth, not Christ.

I see the long-term impact of this when I volunteer at our church's Celebrate Recovery program, which provides a biblical model of recovery for people with hurts, habits, hang-ups, and addictions. When someone grows to a place of health, sometimes they choose to share their story. I delight in hearing these stories of healing, redemption, and recovery. Every story is different, but they all start the same: in childhood. It's terribly normal to hear the decades of struggle that followed a childhood with a drunk father, detached mother, or abusive uncle. People scarred from their childhood cover our planet. Where people live, childhood wounds fester.

Children are surrounded by wounded adults who act in wounded ways, and because children are developmentally impressionable, they soak in whatever we're modeling. When we mishandle our role in what we model for the innocent, we grieve God's heart. God cares for the vulnerable, so he loves children. **God knows that childhood hurts translate into adult dysfunctions, which translate into childhood hurts for the next generation.**

When the collateral damage caused by bunker warfare threatens children, Jesus gets deadly serious: "If anyone causes one of these little ones—those who believe in me—to stumble, it would be better for them if a large millstone were hung around their neck and they were thrown into the sea."[3] Heavy and circular, millstones were used by the ancient world to grind wheat and grain. Some weighed as little as five pounds, but others required the strength of several strong men to move. What a terrible way to die—dragged to the bottom of the sea by a millstone. Jesus made his point: "Do not cause spiritual harm to a child!" (And modeling a bunker mentality is doing just that.)

If people took this warning literally, there would be many more healthy children.

We ought to ask ourselves, "How might I be causing little ones to sin when I respond to those with whom I disagree?" While the list might be endless, let's boil down the possibilities:

1. **You can cause children to sin by what you teach.** If untruthfulness leaks into your teaching, you can cause them to sin. Our culture values personal preference over truth, passivity over love, comfort over sacrifice, and independence over fellowship. Will you teach children the same, or will you teach wisdom and truth, regardless of cultural popularity?

2. **You can cause children to sin by how you live.** By serving on the board of trustees for Blackbox International, which seeks to bring healing to boys rescued from sex trafficking,[4] I have learned about the monstrous behavior of those who traffic children. These people trash lives for a living. I helplessly grieved for months after first hearing of the plight of these boys. It took that season of grieving for me to transition to a place where I could begin thinking about solutions.

   But it doesn't take extreme action to cause a little one to sin. What about an adult's small actions prodding children down the wrong path? What about only praying when it serves yourself?

What about valuing your car more than the poor? What about yelling at your kid as you would a bad pet? What about disrespecting your spouse? Don't these actions also lead children astray?

There's nothing more beautiful than the wide-eyed innocence of children, and there's nothing more tragic than seeing their hearts damaged by the very people to whom God entrusted them. If protecting children was your only reason for leaving your bunker, that would be enough.

// CLOSE OBSERVERS

Someone once asked me if I knew I walked like my dad. I'd never thought about how he walked, and I'd actually never thought about how I walked. (And now that I was thinking about it, walking began to feel awkward and labored.) Later I did some quick math. I figured I'd probably seen my dad take more than one million steps. Plus, when I was little and he was carrying me, I would've even felt him take tens of thousands of steps. It makes sense that I walk like him. It also makes sense that the people closest to you will start to walk like you.

Healthy people tend to be surrounded by lots of other healthy people, and the opposite is also true. We walk like those closest to us. If we choose the ugliness of bunker dwelling, being quick to fight, bite, and smite, some will follow our lead. Our whining will prompt their whining. Our arguing will prompt their arguing. Their lives become our personal collateral damage.

Paul commanded Timothy to walk in a way helpful to those imitating his stride: "Set an example for the believers in speech, in conduct, in love, in faith and in purity."[5] Who's following behind you? They'll imitate your words, actions, attitude, and opinions—so be aware: You might be helping or harming them.

// SPECTATORS

Don't be alarmed, but someone is watching you from a distance. I'm not sure if they're keeping detailed notes in their journal, but

I'm positive they are jotting down some things in their mind. If you claim to be a Christian, and they're not so sure about spiritual things, they're paying especially close attention. Your life is intermingled with their eternity. I don't want to overstate that (God is God and you are you), but I also don't want to understate it. You can make a world of difference.

One time we talked a high school girl into going with our church on a trip to serve the poor. It took a lot of convincing. Her family was a mix of spiritual cynics and seekers, and none were believers. They liked the idea of her helping other people, and my wife and I had spent months building trust, so they decided to let her go. She did great on the trip, but she distanced herself from us after the trip. While on the trip, unbeknownst to me, she was the victim of two other girls' meanness. They talked behind her back and to her face. She didn't want to make a big deal of it, so she just walked away. Six years later, she called me out of the blue. She was in trouble and needed to talk. She told me how her teenage years unfolded tragically and how her adult life was full of misery and trouble. She'd tried to fill her soul with the love of a man who treated her like garbage.

I can't blame a week of meanness from two girls for all of her troubles, but I also can't ignore the collateral damage it caused. Those girls were being watched, and Jesus was being judged by their actions. What if these girls would've loved this "outsider" with the love of Christ? What if she would've embraced the love God had for her? What if she'd known how God valued her? What if she'd known that the approval of a man could never satisfy her soul?

God knew many "outsiders" would judge the gospel based on how the "insiders" lived. It's why he commanded things like "Live an exemplary life among the natives so that your actions will refute their prejudices. Then they'll be won over to God's side and be there to join in the celebration when he arrives."[6]

Before you speak, act, or post an opinion online, remember that someone far from God is watching you.

// OURSELVES

Lastly, when we live in a bunker, we hurt ourselves. Imagine a grenade so heavy that you can throw it far enough to wound others, but not far enough for you to escape harm. The very act of launching an attack slashes the joy, peace, and love God offers to your soul. And don't forget what's likely to happen if you attack someone—they'll attack back.

Even if they don't attack back, harm is done. If I hurt someone else, intentionally or not, I've damaged the chances of being a positive influence in their life. When I've proven I don't care about truth, I can no longer be trusted. When I've proven I don't care about people, I can no longer be trusted. To live life as an untrustworthy person is a terrible thing.

Consider the fulfillment you find in offering words of guidance and wisdom to someone looking up to you. Consider the sense of purpose you feel when a grieving friend comes to you for a comforting hug. God gave you the infinitely rewarding joy of helping other people. Don't reject that gift.

LIES

"My life only impacts me" is a lie bubbling from the pits of hell. We want to believe this lie because it alleviates guilt, excusing our envy and malice. We don't seek to cause collateral damage, but it happens nonetheless if we reject the difficult work called "change." So we're tempted, instead, to try to soothe our consciences by believing our lives never affect others: children, neighbors, family, friends, strangers, ourselves.

The truth is, none of us lives in a vacuum. Our actions and words—good or bad—reverberate through our families, churches, and communities for generations. This is terrifying . . . but also wonderful. We don't have to leave destruction in our wake. We can spur on blessings instead of collateral damage, goodwill instead of revenge, friends instead of foes. What a beautiful sight that would be.

REFLECTION QUESTIONS

1. When have you been "unintentionally" wounded by others living in a bunker?

2. Why does Jesus speak so sternly to those who cause harm to children?

3. Who's following you, watching how you walk through life? What do you think they are learning from you?

4. List three people (or groups of people) who might be watching you from a distance. Is that a good thing for them?

5. Have you honestly owned the influence you have in the lives of others?

CHAPTER 4

FRIEND OR FOE

The thief comes only to steal and kill and destroy.
JOHN 10:10

AIDED BY THE COVER OF DARKNESS, the Australian Fiftieth Infantry Battalion pushed toward the German trenches in the Battle of Villers-Bretonneux on April 24, 1918. Despite heavy gunfire, they pressed on. As they neared the trenches, someone cried an order to bomb the trenches.

Grenades flew through the air. Crawls turned into runs. And soon, the soldiers were killing and were being killed by the enemy in the trench.

Except . . . they weren't fighting the enemy. There were no German soldiers in the trench—only British soldiers, unaware help was coming. The Australians assumed Germans were attacking. The allies killed one another.

Around seventy-five thousand French soldiers died during World War I as a result of friendly fire.[1] Friendly fire adds to the death toll of any war, but it also sabotages the spirit of the survivors. Even strong men crumple at the horror of being inadvertently attacked by their own friends.

It hurts to be harshly criticized by a distant friend or complete stranger, but you probably won't lose any sleep that night. However, the harsh criticism of a spouse or close friend may wound you for nights, weeks, or years. Spilling your two-dollar bowl of nachos is a bummer, but watching your hand-built house go up in flames devastates. The more we invest in something, the more we care about it: "For where your treasure is, there your heart will be also."[2] And the more we rely on the comfort and care of a friend, the more it hurts when they turn their back—or even worse, their weapons—on us. Friendly fire hurts worse than any other attack.

That's why the first rule of battle is to know your enemy. Military strategists revere *The Art of War* by Sun Tzu, a Chinese general and philosopher who lived around 500 BC. He wrote, "If you know the enemy and know yourself, you need not fear the result of a hundred battles. If you know yourself but not the enemy, for every victory gained you will also suffer a defeat."[3]

If you've chosen to live in the bunkers, I have gut-wrenching news: You are aiming your weapon at the wrong person. You're mistaken about whom your enemy is.

THE REAL ENEMY

No person is your enemy. Seriously. Not one. Not your ex-spouse, a back-stabbing coworker, a slanderous classmate, a greedy boss, a crooked politician, a deadbeat dad, or the driver who just cut you off in traffic. As believers, we might be tempted to say that anyone who is not a Christian is our enemy, but that's just more bunker thinking. We need to be clear-sighted about who really wants to pit us against each other, whether we follow Christ or not. Ephesians 6:12 depicts the spiritual battle we face:

> Our struggle is not against flesh and blood, but against the rulers, against the authorities, against the powers of this dark world and against the spiritual forces of evil in the heavenly realms.

Oh, if we would believe this verse! If we really believed it, this whole book would be unnecessary. Our true enemy is not clothed in skin. He delights when we try to destroy each other, because it makes his job so much easier:

> Your enemy the devil prowls around like a roaring lion looking for someone to devour.
>
> I PETER 5:8

As long as we view each other as the enemy, he wins. When a married couple views each other as enemies, reconciliation is futile. When two employees view each other as enemies, their productivity is crippled. When two Christians view each other as enemies, God's intentions are hindered. And when government officials view each other as enemies, partisan politics rule the day.

The reality is, the devil loves to see us fighting each other. If you view any human as your enemy, you're playing right into the devil's hands. But if we recognize how and why we make enemies, we can begin to lower our voices and fists.

WEAPONS OF FRIENDLY FIRE

The enemy uses many weapons to divide us and conquer us, and he's glad to let you borrow any of them. Things like gossip, jealousy, and false teaching serve his purpose well.

Imagine if you and I were great friends. (I hope it's not hard for you to do.) Imagine we enjoyed hiking, serving at the church's food pantry, and eating barbecue together. As the mayor's election neared, imagine I found out that you were supporting the lady who was running as an Independent, but I was supporting the Whig Party candidate (okay, that's a stretch, but bear with me). If I began telling people that you didn't care for the homeless people in our city because your candidate hadn't made it a major talking point, you'd be inclined to label me as your enemy. If left unresolved, your mistrust and disrespect would grow.

You may not have even noticed if my attack was intentional or not—it's hard to care when you're ducking for cover.

The weapons used in my silly example are weapons used in real life every day: dishonesty, slander, hate, etc. They are often more subtle and used in a passive-aggressive way. They often distort. They always lead to harm, intentional or not.

// INTENTIONAL ATTACK

When I crouch in a bunker, I identify anyone outside the bunker as an enemy. Bunkers create separation. You are either my friend or my foe. And one way we foment the us-versus-them mentality is through gossip. Gossip flourishes in bunkers. Gossips want to snare your loyalty, to entice you to join their bunker and add their enemy to your hit list. When someone wrinkles their face, shakes their head, and says, "Did you hear what Reggie did?" I hope you'll picture them gesturing for you to hop into their bunker—the one where everyone talks bad about Reggie.

Proverbs 16:28 warns us that "a gossip separates close friends." Think about those implications! Good friends are hard to come by. It might take years of fostering a deeply close friendship—yet gossip can blow it all to smithereens. God is deeply concerned about the sources of division, and he orders us to censor one of those sources, gossip, before it can escape our lips. With the amount of attention the Bible gives to gossip, you would hope the church never struggled with it. But all too often, passionate people find themselves emotionally overinvested, spiritually immature, and living in close quarters. Because they refuse to grow up and manage their passions, they gossip about their brothers and sisters in Christ.

When gossip infects the troops, distrust grows and armies splinter. It may be framed as an innocent observation or helpful tidbit, but it's much more—gossip is a dangerous, intentional, peace-wrecking sin.

// BAD INTEL

Sometimes we share bad information, not out of evil intent, but out of misunderstanding. But even well-intended (or so we think) friendly fire destroys.

Several years ago, our church launched a major ministry initiative. Several of the key leaders committed to fasting and praying during the day of the weekly event. I loved this and joined them when possible.

We soon discovered that some were physically incapable of performing their exhausting ministry roles if they spent the day without food. When they brought this to me, I suggested they consider fasting on another day, if needed. I desired to encourage their fasting but also to express God's grace with spiritual disciplines.

Unfortunately, a good friend received a terribly inaccurate interpretation of my words. He believed I discouraged the team from fasting. Period. Of course, this was nowhere near my desire. I doubt anyone tried to make him think poorly of me, but that's exactly what happened.

My friend grew distant . . . for years.

One day, after trying to get together with him for months, I finally succeeded. He shared the information he'd received four years earlier.

Four years! Four years of festering. Four years of believing something untrue.

Like most stories, there's more to this than one misinterpretation. But I wonder how the story would go if we both had known the truth all along. What if he'd known what I actually said? What if I'd known what he heard and thought? When people think you undercut them, they will doubt your motives for everything you do. It clouds their reality and yours. My friend thought I was treating him more as a foe than a friend.

We will always encounter misinterpretations in life, whether of something we said or of something we heard. That's why we must have conversations. Admit hurts. Ask questions. Hear explanations. Perhaps there is more to the story, or perhaps an apology will surface. And in stepping through the misunderstanding to find the truth, we can turn an enemy back into a friend.

// THE WORST WEAPON

As bad as gossip and misunderstanding are, one weapon has more capacity to inflict long-term pain and harm than both combined. Some accuse

Christians of using the Bible as a crutch, but worse could be said—over the years, some have used it to attack others. Using Scripture as a weapon against others involves twisting it in a way God never intended, using God's words to dehumanize and strike at others. It's a horrific use of something that is supposed to be life-giving.

The American Civil War produced the worst examples of using Scripture in such a horrific way. Prior to the 1820s, many Baptists in the North and South opposed slavery, reflective of larger views in the South at that time, a legacy of a pre-cotton economy. But by the mid-1840s, Baptist sentiment in the South—at least as expressed in denominational leadership—agreed God had ordained enslavement.

Denominational church leader Richard Furman aligned with John Leland, a prominent minister. As pressure mounted from the South, both men began championing the rights of slave owners. For Leland, this was a dramatic change of mind. He once spoke against slavery. Now, he defended the "peculiar institution," endorsing the words of Furman.

Furman, while president of the 1823 South Carolina State Convention of Baptists, wrote on behalf of South Carolina Baptists to the governor. His letter, a response to an attempted slave uprising the previous year, is considered a watershed event in the beginning of a movement toward consolidation of white Baptists in the South to the pro-slavery position:

> Certain writers on politics, morals and religion, and some
> of them highly respectable, have advanced positions, and
> inculcated sentiments, very unfriendly to the principle
> and practice of holding slaves. . . . These sentiments, the
> Convention, on whose behalf I address your Excellency,
> cannot think just, or well founded; for the right of holding
> slaves is clearly established in the Holy Scriptures, both by
> precept and example.[4]

While nearly two more decades would pass before the sentiments of white South Carolina Baptists were fully realized among Baptists of the

South at large, the die had been cast: Baptists in America were on the road to formal division over the issue of slavery.[5]

My heart breaks to see how people used the Bible as a blunt-force weapon against African Americans and abolitionists.[6] But I reject the conclusion that such examples require us to abandon the Bible. I believe, instead, they require us to quit misusing the Bible—cramming the Bible's words under our prejudice rather than submitting to its words.

If you live in a bunker, you will use and misuse whatever you can find as a weapon. As long as it causes damage to others and makes you feel more secure, it's fair game.

LOVED ONES

Knowing who our friends are is the best way to stand against our enemy. Have you ever tried to make a list of all your friends, all your loved ones? I don't know how long your list would be, but I hope you don't forget these four:

// 1. THE BIBLE

The Bible is indeed intended to be a weapon, but not one with which to attack other people. The Bible is a spiritual weapon,[7] meant to destroy the barrage of lies, temptations, guilt, and hurt fired by the devil. It's also our friend. The other day our family was silently reading Proverbs 26 as we ate breakfast. As several of us came to verse 21 at the same time, we let out audible gasps: "As charcoal to embers and as wood to fire, so is a quarrelsome person for kindling strife." Can you guess what was happening right before we started reading? Quarrels. I never cease to be amazed at how relevant Scripture is. It may be ancient, but it's also time-less, and it's the best resource I've ever seen for learning to navigate life. One verse leaped off the page and made us rethink what we were doing just minutes earlier. That's the power of the Bible. It's a powerful friend.

I've noticed the more people read the Bible, the more they love it. David's love for God's Word is put on full display in the Psalms. He says he delights in the Scriptures. It sounds as if he's talking about his best friend.

When the Bible becomes our friend and we love God's Word so much that it shapes our lives, we learn how to be family, friends, church, community. We believe the story of God, we realize the story of evil, and we embrace the story God has called us to live. God's Word is living and active, and I pray it will be your friend.

// 2. GOD

I'd expect the God of the universe to call me a servant or slave. That seems fair, even though I don't deserve to have any relationship with him. But God goes way beyond that. He calls us his children, even his friends.

Maybe you don't have many friends. I hope that changes, but I also hope you know that no friend on the planet can be as reliable, trustworthy, and wonderful as God.

If you want to know what kind of friend God is, read Matthew, Mark, Luke, and John and see how Jesus was a friend. He did everything a friend—a perfect friend—would do. He comforted, he gave his time, he helped, he listened, and he told his friends what was good for them to know.

Have you ever pictured God as a cosmic disciplinarian, quick to lash out at anyone who fails him? If so, you may have come to view God more as a foe than as a friend. As we read the Bible, our picture of God adjusts, just as if you were to look at the Grand Canyon from four different edges. Every perspective reveals different realities. Yes, God is all-powerful, and yes, he hates evil. But he's also merciful, kind, and quick to forgive. When we rightly view God with reverence and respect, we also see how God likes us. He wants to spend time with us, as a friend.

// 3. YOU

I often hear people say, "I'm my own worst enemy." They might say this after staying out too late and oversleeping the morning of a final exam. I understand the sentiment of the phrase, but it's not actually true. You may not be helping yourself and your goals, but there's someone capable of causing you even more harm. Ephesians 6 doesn't list you as the enemy. There's a spiritual war going on, and you're in the middle of it.

Since God created you, your life is highly valued. Jesus would do anything and everything for you—in fact, he already has.

You may be living like a fool, but God still values you. You need to learn to value yourself too. You aren't the enemy. You are loved.

// 4. EVERYONE ELSE

If you said you loved me, but I saw you push my little daughter off her bicycle, I wouldn't believe you (and some other things might happen too). You can't mistreat my kids and love me. It's impossible. To love me necessitates that you love my children. God thinks the same: "By this everyone will know that you are my disciples, if you love one another."[8] You can't love God and hate his children, his creations, his love.

Just as you are valuable because God made you and Jesus died for you, so is every other human on this planet. Like them or not, God loves them. They aren't your enemies. God hopes you'll be friends. He yearns for brotherly love and sisterly hugs between you and that person who used to be your enemy. (Note the past tense. It may take a while, but work at it, pray about it. We'll help you more with this later in the book.)

God loves every person and longs to be everyone's friend. And God loves you. He's never been your enemy. He knows who the enemy is. Do you?

REFLECTION QUESTIONS

1. Why are we so quick to make enemies?

2. Does someone view you as their enemy? Why?

3. Which of the four "loved ones" do you need to view as a friend and not as the enemy?

4. Whom have you mislabeled as "enemy"? Will you commit to no longer viewing them as an enemy? This may take work and help from others, but it begins with your commitment.

CHAPTER 5

ARE YOU IN A BUNKER?

———

Blessed is the one who does not walk in step with the wicked or stand in the way that sinners take or sit in the company of mockers.

PSALM 1:1

COMEDIAN JEFF FOXWORTHY entertained millions with his self-deprecating "You might be a redneck if . . ." routine. He poked fun at his own culture with quips such as "If someone asked to see your ID and you showed them your belt buckle, yooouuu might be a redneck." Everyone with a giant "Roy," "Slim," or other name etched on their buckle loved Foxworthy's jokes because his words revealed peculiar things about themselves that they'd never thought about before. Good comedians hold up a giant mirror to the audience and make them laugh about the funny things they do.

God also holds a giant mirror before us, but not to garner a chuckle. He wants to help us see our value, strengths, weaknesses, and flaws. Scripture reading and reflection help us see ourselves in a new light. If God's Word really is living and active, and I believe it is, it has the power to show us things we've never seen. If the Holy Spirit is in your life, he doesn't intend to leave you alone. He desires to both encourage and convict. He'll show you truth and then hold up a mirror so you can look at the differences between the two. Wise friends, insightful spouses, innocent children, convicting sermons, good books, and thoughtful songs can also help us see ourselves for who we really are—and where we really are.

We'll spend the rest of this chapter looking in the mirror, because do you know what is worse than knowingly living in a bunker? Living in a bunker . . . and not knowing it. Ignorance means you can't even begin to address the issue. Maybe you're convinced that's not you. Maybe you're thinking, *C'mon. I don't mistreat other people. I'm fine!* But we all need to be cautious about assuming we're above this way of living.

Do you have the courage to honestly look in the mirror?

YOU MIGHT BE IN A BUNKER IF . . .

// . . . YOU RAIN DOWN FIRE

In Jesus' day, the Jews considered the Samaritans to be the enemy, the outcasts, the half-breeds, and plenty of other derogatory terms. Jesus lambasted this prejudice with both words and actions, but it took a long time for such a scandalous teaching to work its way into the hearts of his followers.

One day when they were traveling through Samaria, Jesus sent a few of his disciples ahead to find a place where they could eat and rest. Culturally, only one thing was unusual about this request: Jesus and his disciples were Jews, and they were asking Samaritans for help. Even though Jesus had specifically reached out to Samaritans, the people in this town had rejected the request. The disciples were irate. Not only had they been rejected, they'd been rejected by Samaritans, "less-thans." Jesus had worked so hard to bridge the divide, but clearly the battle lines were once again drawn. Because the Samaritans had retreated to their bunker, surely the Jewish followers of Jesus should retreat to theirs, too. Two of Jesus' closest disciples, James and John, had an idea about what Jesus should do to these hostile villagers:

> "Lord, do you want us to call fire down from heaven to destroy them?" But Jesus turned and rebuked them.
>
> LUKE 9:54-55

I doubt James and John had much experience calling down fire, but they knew Jesus could make it happen. They'd have loved to see those Samaritans burn, but Jesus slammed the door on their idea. I wish Luke would've included the details of Jesus' rebuke. Maybe he made them suffer through an hour-long diatribe. Maybe he spoke one loud word. Maybe he gave them a look they'd never forget. Regardless of how he rebuked them, his message stung: "I'm not joining your bunker, your hate. I love the Samaritans, too." Little did the disciples know that Jesus would soon be forgiving attacks far worse than a dinner snub.

Can I give a modern-day translation of what James and John felt about the Samaritans? "To h— with you!" You don't have to speak it out loud to say it in your heart. You say it when you wish harm on another person. You say it when you dismiss a group of people you dislike. You say it when you quit caring about another person's soul. If you are "calling down fire" on another person, you're deep in a bunker. I'm not sure how he'd do it, but Jesus would rebuke you.

// ... YOU AMASS TROOPS

The more people you count in your bunker, the safer you'll feel. You may not actually *be* safer, but when we're in a crowd, all believing and doing the same things, it feels reassuring. This is why those in a bunker try to recruit others to join them. Every added person means there's one less enemy on the other side and a little more firepower on your side.

One day I remember being recruited to join a fight. I came to the gas station in peace, but peace, as it turns out, wasn't in the cards.

A mom and daughter pulled up to pump number seven in the middle of a disagreement that had clearly begun years before. The daughter, about seventeen, slammed her passenger door and pierced the morning quiet with a sharp "Fine. I'll get the gas."

It was obvious she had never pumped gas before. She fumbled with a credit card and then could not figure out how to get the "stuff" into the "thing" (her words).

Her mom sneered out the window, "You think you're so smart, but now look at you!"

Typically, I like to help someone who's struggling with a simple task, especially when they are only about ten feet away. I've been there—I've struggled with plenty of simple tasks myself. But jumping into the middle of this family feud seemed like the worst possible idea.

The slam of the car door announced that the mom's patience was over. She grabbed the pump, lifted the handle, and started filling it up. Moments later, her daughter frantically screamed, "Mom, stop! Stop the gas! I can't afford five dollars!"

And that's when it happened . . .

The mom's glare shifted from her daughter to me. Right at me. She asked me, "Can you believe this?"

I knew what she was doing. She wanted support. She wanted me to help her chastise and belittle her daughter. She wanted me to join her bunker.

Meanwhile, I was silently rehearsing, *No hablo inglés.* Sometimes you just gotta do whatever it takes to avoid the fray.

At the gas station, an invitation to join an argument was an invitation to join a hate club. If you get an invite to join the KKK, you'd know why they want you to join. They want you to hate other human beings. But have you been asking, prompting, pressuring people to join you in your own bunkers? And if they were to join you, would that naturally lead them to despise others? Would agreeing with what you think about Aunt Mary cause them to dislike Aunt Mary? Would going along with your thoughts about politics persuade them to despise a neighbor or anonymous thousands of people they've never met?

If you manipulate, exaggerate, and find yourself obsessing about trying to get people on your side of an argument, you're in a bunker. Your desire to help people see The Truth has been swallowed by your need to convince people to agree with Your Truth.

// . . . YOU'RE NEVER PERSUADED TO CHANGE

I have a hard time believing that every single thing you believed a decade ago was spot-on. Surely one of your political, theological, or relational beliefs was at least slightly skewed. So if decades come and go but not a single one of your thoughts changes, it means one of two things: Either you're the golden child, or you're in a bunker. If you never change, you're not open to change. Don't get me wrong—I don't want your faith in God or your love of family to waver, but I'd expect you to at least moderately change your mind on what the best political solution is to any given problem, or how you can be a better parent, or why God might speak more or less strongly about a biblical issue than you once thought.

Saul of Tarsus, later called Paul, was a man of conviction, clout, and passion. However, his convictions were completely wrong. He thought Christianity was a lie and thus a threat to God's will. His mission in life was to catch, imprison, and, when necessary, kill Christians.

If ever a man was in a bunker, it was Paul, but a supernatural experience revealed to him that Jesus really was the Son of God. Sometimes we rush past this moment in the story. Lots of people have been confronted with the truth, yet they refused it. Perhaps Paul remembered how many times Pharaoh refused God's obvious messages to him as he oppressed and enslaved the Israelite nation. Perhaps he remembered how King Ahab saw God do an amazing miracle, and yet he returned to his wicked ways. Paul did not repeat the mistakes of the proud bunker dwellers who refused to change. Acts 9 tells how he followed God's instructions, listened to a believer explain the gospel, and was baptized—dying to his old way of life and being raised up as a new creation.

God persuaded Paul to leave his bunker. Has he persuaded you to leave any of yours? Are you changing, growing, and open to correction?

> Those who disregard discipline despise themselves, but the one who heeds correction gains understanding.
>
> PROVERBS 15:32

Here are a few more simple signs you may be in a bunker:

- **You only listen to and read from sources that agree with you.** For the arrogant husband, this means talking only to people who will go along with your disrespect of your wife. For the politically minded, this means you only read sources reinforcing your positions.

- **You lack friends who disagree with your spiritual or political beliefs.** Do you avoid people who think differently than you? Have you offended them, causing them to avoid you? Do your opinions raise barriers to relationships?

- **Your anger over differences with others overpowers your compassion for their souls.** Does love or anger dominate your deepest feelings about others?

- **When people leave your presence, they're likely worked up about an issue.** Do you add fuel to divisive, unimportant issues, or do you add calm and proper perspective? Do you take every opportunity to bring up divisive subjects?

- **You have the same conversation, over and over, with the same people, about the same topic.** Do you find comfort in digging deeper with like-minded friends? Do those with different opinions avoid you?

- **You either demonize or idolize others.** Do you gloss over foolish behavior from those who support your causes? Do you quickly spot your enemy's shortcomings, while rushing to defend your own failures and the failures of your friends? Have you despised a political figure during the primary, but after they won your party's nomination begun to gloss over their flaws?

- **You spread information without any concern for its accuracy or helpfulness.** Do you share Internet stories, without regard for truth, as long as they fit your agenda?

- **You say things that get half-hearted, awkward, or silent responses in return.** When people don't want to pick a fight but also don't want to affirm your harsh, ignorant words, they'll stay real quiet.

Saying, "I like George Clooney, even though he's such a crazy liberal" escalates the discomfort level of a room.[1] Do you assume everyone agrees with you about everything?

- **You often begin statements with "I'm sorry, but . . ." followed by derogatory remarks.** No, you are not sorry; you are angry. You lack self-control and compassion.

- **You have a martyr complex.** Ever notice how feuding spouses, fighting friends, and warring politicians all feel as if they are the victims?

- **Your family or friends believe that if they do not agree with your position, your relationship will be intensely difficult.** They force a smile and nod.

- **When your position suffers a victory or setback, it affects your attitude and emotions for hours, days, or weeks on end.** What causes you to rejoice or mourn? Did Jesus rejoice or mourn about similar things?

Enter a bunker and you may find protection, but you'll be forced to fire bullets, too. The moment you join a bunker, you cut the communication lines with anyone else. You lose any capacity to speak to opposing views.

John Piper, in his book on race relations, bemoans how those trying to build unity between different ethnic groups always face criticism for their imperfect efforts, which often leads them to give up altogether.[2] Perhaps you have experienced this yourself as you tried to bring peace to your family or friends.

Do not give up. You can stand by your principles without attacking from a bunker. It has been done. It's *being* done. You can do this. We can do this together.

To put a stop to your bunker living will require you to move, crawl, climb, and even dance. The only way to *stop living where you are* is to *go somewhere new.* Heroes climb out of bunkers, but they find a strange, foreign land. I hope you'll go there with me.

REFLECTION QUESTIONS

1. What are the three biggest feuds you see in your world?

2. Are you guilty of wanting to "call down fire" on someone?

3. What bunkers have you entered?

4. How have bunkers damaged your life? How have they damaged the lives of those around you?

5. Are you committed to learning a new way?

PART II

NO MAN'S LAND

Then something Tookish woke up inside him, and he wished to go and see the great mountains, and hear the pine-trees and the waterfalls, and explore the caves, and wear a sword instead of a walking-stick. He looked out of the window. The stars were out in a dark sky above the trees. He thought of the jewels of the dwarves shining in dark caverns. Suddenly in the wood beyond The Water a flame leapt up—probably somebody lighting a wood-fire—and he thought of plundering dragons settling on his quiet Hill and kindling it all to flames. He shuddered; and very quickly he was plain Mr. Baggins of Bag-End, Under-Hill, again.

He got up trembling.

J. R. R. TOLKIEN, *The Hobbit*

CHAPTER 6

DAUNTING AND INVITING

———

What one does when faced with the truth is more difficult than you think.

WONDER WOMAN

A FEW YEARS AGO some close friends and I decided we needed a physical challenge. We'd committed to growing in the Lord together, and we decided we wanted to raise money for Blackbox International by running/climbing/crawling the Warrior Dash. The Warrior Dash combines a 5K trail run, twelve obstacles, and lots of mud. The more we thought about it, the more we liked the idea of suffering, if only a little bit, in order to help boys who've suffered so much.

So we started training. After each jog, we'd text each other an update:

> I ran less than a mile in twelve minutes. I had to stop every three to four minutes to rest.

> I ran a half mile but had to stop, because, um, I felt like my dog needed a break.

> I ran one mile and hated every step.

We weren't exactly destined for greatness. But we kept training, changed our eating habits, and asked people to support our cause. We were highly motivated to finish.

When the day arrived, we excitedly but cautiously made our way down the path, over the walls, and through ditches. Finally, we arrived at the signature obstacle, the Muddy Mayhem. A one-hundred-foot mud pit with barbed wire stretched across every few yards lay between us and the finish line. Army crawling was the only way to conquer it. We could see people struggling in the pit. They were losing shoes, spitting out mud, wiping their eyes, and moving as slowly as you'd expect. To make matters worse, my friend Alan said, "That mud reminds me of some diapers I've changed. Who knows what's in there." But on the other side, people were crossing the finish line, high-fiving, dancing, and hugging.

You can't think about these things too long. The longer you do, the harder it is to take the plunge. So we gave each other a look, nodded, and dived into the filth. I remember questioning why we'd ever thought this was a good idea, but looking at my friends made the struggle at least slightly fun. We eventually made it and joined others in celebrating.

There are times when the path in front of us looks daunting because of the resistance we face. When you're choosing to step out of the bunkers, two realities can adjust your vision to see the path as more inviting than daunting:

1. You're already in the mud; you're just not moving yet.
2. Dancing and hugging are in your future.

CHOOSING

Staying out of bunkers means jumping into a radical way of life. It may feel as if you're crawling through mud at times, but the journey is worth it. While we're going to unpack the vital principles of this peace-and-truth life in the rest of part 2, let's look at two important pieces to keep in mind before we go forward.

// 1. CHOOSING NOT TO CHOOSE

The first radical way to walk out of bunkers and toward freedom is to choose not to take a side. It sounds simple when I say it like that, but it's anything but simple. This place in the middle, this decision to walk in truth without choosing a bunker, is what we'll call *no man's land.*

On the battlefield, no man's land is the exposed area between two bunkers. It offers neither concealment nor protection. Soldiers ordered to charge onto it know death is likely. Soldiers wounded there may wait days for rescue. No man's land is the last place in the world a soldier wants to be.[1] Yet, in everyday life, humble pioneers call no man's land home.

The late Reverend E. V. Hill once found himself in no man's land.[2] He once spoke about a time when he received death threats from both the Ku Klux Klan and the Black Panthers, two opposing groups, both entrenched. Hill was working with Martin Luther King Jr. to promote civil rights and racial reconciliation. Like King, he refused to lock arms with anyone favoring violence. He chose to walk the middle way, and in doing so, he made enemies. But making people happy wasn't his goal. Reconciliation, justice, and hope were his goals. Hill chose to live in no man's land, dangerous as it was.

When people want us to choose sides, the pressure gets intense. They're not politely asking. If we decline their offer, they'll take it as a personal rejection.

We are left with a great dilemma:

Do I side with them and thus reject someone else?

Or do I refuse them, leaving them feeling rejected (and apt to reject me)?

Whether it's an international incident, a political issue, or a dispute between your neighbors, you're going to feel the pressure to pick a side. So how should you handle this when it comes up? How do you choose to step into no man's land? Speaking calmly and gently under pressure doesn't come naturally or easily. But it can be done. What if, during heated situations, instead of attacks we heard things like

- "Well, we should wait and learn more about it before forming an opinion."
- "I am trying to understand both sides fully."
- "I have a clear opinion on this issue, but posting it on social media may not be the best way to engage people."
- "This whole issue is really not important at all, so I'll focus my thoughts elsewhere."
- "I respectfully disagree. Here is why . . . Do you see where I am coming from? Help me understand you."

// 2. CHOOSING BOTH GOOD THINGS

The second radical way to walk toward freedom is to pursue two biblical principles at the same time, even when they appear—at first blush—to contradict each other. If you want to live in no man's land, you must never pursue one principle at the expense of another. In each case, they must work together. This dance proves to be more difficult than you might imagine.

Here's an example. The Bible instructs parents to be kind to their children. God desires for parents to give their children a glimpse of his extravagant kindness. The Bible also instructs parents to discipline their children and to not spoil them. God knew that parents would be prone to swoop in and rescue their kids at every first sign of trouble, preventing their children from learning responsibility. So should parents choose kindness or discipline? Of course, the answer is both.

Beth and I hate getting a call from our children's school. We love the school, but we know that the call might be one of our kids. They might tell us they aren't feeling well, but they are probably telling us that they forgot their lunch. So we have a choice to make: kindness or discipline? Will I drop everything in my busy day to bring them lunch, or will I say, "(1) Where is the emergency five dollars you're supposed to keep hidden in your locker for such a time as this? (2) This has happened before and your friends shared their extra food with you, so start begging them. (3) I bet you'll remember your lunch tomorrow. (4) You'll thank me someday. (5) Love you!" (That last one spoken in an overly happy voice, of course.)

I've chosen both options with my kids. If I knew my son probably forgot his lunch because he was having a tough week, or because he was busy helping his little sister carry her science project to the car, I'd drop everything and take him lunch. But if he'd forgotten his lunch multiple times that month, he'd better hope his friends don't eat the crusts of their sandwiches.

With my children, when I lean toward kindness, I hope I still value discipline. And when I lean toward discipline, I hope I do so with kindness. God wants me to pursue both, and sometimes that feels like a dance.

God never contradicts himself. Instead, he balances us. We're tempted to choose one worthy pursuit at the expense of others, but God invites us to choose both. He invites us to choose swampy trails over concrete walls, nuanced convictions over dogmatic extremes. He invites us to say yes to all good things, never pitting one against the other.

DODGING AND DANCING

Imagine if, when my son forgot his lunch, I chose kindness. And imagine when I pulled into the school parking lot, lunch in hand, a crowd of angry protesters greeted me, waving signs with "Quit spoiling your children" or "Proverbs 29:17" written on them. And then imagine that a counterprotest showed up, chanting, "Parents who say no, to hell they go!" What would I do? What if I don't like either extreme?

I hope I'd find the courage to walk between the two groups. If they started throwing things at me, I'd duck, swoop, and swerve. If you saw me from a distance, you might think I was dancing, but I might only be dodging.

You've never seen a riot caused by your son forgetting his lunch, but I bet you've felt the fear of being surrounded by warring opponents. Perhaps you've dodged accusations from one side that you don't care enough for a needy friend, and from the other that you're unwisely giving too much money away. When those accusations come at the same time, the space between can feel pretty lonely. It feels like a no man's land.

Dwelling in no man's land necessitates the shedding of comfort, pride, and habit. Something will get slaughtered in our travels: either our adversaries or our pride. Which of the two will you let die?

Despite the coming onslaught, noble men and women traverse the dangers of this untamed, yet beautiful, wilderness. They go. They hope to die that others might live. But their death is the way to life. As we learn from them, we'll clothe ourselves with the virtues of peace.

In no man's land, these virtues are the tensions that help us navigate the war raging around us. The main tension, the one that informs all the others, is learning to balance grace and truth in order to avoid the temptations of bunkers. All our other responses emerge from this fundamental pairing. We must learn to speak with wisdom and tact, to act with both gentleness and strength, to allow our conviction to be seasoned with nuance, to be both innocent and shrewd, and to show both humility and courage.

It may seem like a tall order, but as we follow Christ, he will show us the way forward. He'll show us we're not alone. If people see us, it may look as if we're only dodging, but we're actually learning to dance.

REFLECTION QUESTIONS

1. Does walking toward no man's land, away from the figurative bunkers in our world, look more daunting or inviting to you?

2. Do you think you've pursued a biblical principle at the expense of another? How so?

3. When do you feel the uncertainty of not knowing which good thing/biblical principle to pursue?

4. When have you felt attacked by opposing sides?

5. Are you willing to begin exploring the biblical principles God has called you to pursue? Are you open to change?

CHAPTER 7

GRACE AND TRUTH

Truth without love is brutality and love without truth is hypocrisy.
WARREN W. WIERSBE

IN JOHN 8, Pharisees interrupted Jesus' teaching by dragging a woman in front of him. They'd caught her committing adultery, and they wanted to stone her for it. (Meanwhile, the guilty man walked free.)

The Pharisees were thirsting for blood. They pretended to aim their attack at the woman, but it was Jesus who was caught in their crosshairs. They intended to trap him, forcing him to choose an extreme position—to step into their bunker, or to set himself firmly against them by choosing a different bunker. Gripping rocks in their hands, they asked, "Shouldn't we honor God by punishing this woman for her sin? Yes or no?" They presented Jesus with an *either/or*, but he chose *neither*. He chose no man's land.

Jesus bent down and began scribbling in the dirt. Perhaps he listed their sins, wrote the name of the guilty man, or quoted Scripture. We're not sure. But from the lonely wilds of no man's land, he offered a challenge: "Let any one of you who is without sin be the first to throw a stone at her."

Thud. Thud. Thud.

The sound of rocks hitting the ground broke the silence. Foiled again. Dejected, the Pharisees walked away defeated, a familiar experience for those trying to trap Jesus.

Jesus looked at the woman. "Where are they? Has no one condemned you?"

"No one, sir."

"Then neither do I condemn you."

Jesus refused to join her accusers. He rejected their bait. He rejected their hate. He emphasized *grace*.

But the story isn't over. Because then he emphasized *truth*.

"Go now and leave your life of sin." His parting words would surely echo in her heart.

Jesus rejected both the accusers' sinful lust for judgment *and* the sin of adultery. Everyone was redirected to see Jesus as judge. The Pharisees saw how much Jesus valued people, even those they detested. The woman, saved by Jesus' grace, saw how much Jesus valued God's commands—truth. We get to see the powerful combination of grace and truth at work. And grace and truth, working together in harmony, lead us into the beautiful danger of no man's land.

LOVE IS THE TENSION

It's common to find people who separate grace and truth, but Jesus never does. If we're going to choose to walk into no man's land, we must embrace them both. Henry Cloud wrote, "In the same way that Truth (without grace) can be called Judgment, Grace (without truth) can be named License [to sin]."[1]

We can, of course, misuse both grace and truth in a variety of ways. James Emery White diagrammed the four options we have when it comes to grace and truth, and only one of those options leads us out of the bunkers.[2]

Option 1 reflects hopelessness. Think of a bystander to the John 8 story shrugging and saying, "I don't care if the adulterous woman is

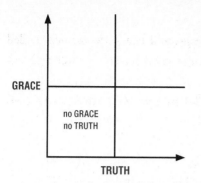

killed, but I also don't care that she committed adultery." No truth + no grace = I don't care. White placed Buddhism, with its generic treatment of truth, in this quadrant. Jesus, however, got real specific: "I am the way and the truth and the life."[3]

Proponents of Option 1 may throw in the towel altogether. What point is there? Why keep trying? Why even think about it anymore?

Option 2 lures people into a palatable, easy Christianity. It glosses over the guilt caused by sin, fearing that truth will scare people away from God. But if you diminish sin, you also diminish grace. White noted, "If you have grace, but no truth, you have licentiousness. In other words, almost anything goes in terms of life or thought. This is the 'cheap grace' that Dietrich Bonhoeffer lamented so famously in his classic, *The Cost of Discipleship*."[4] We are left asking, "If sin's not so bad, why did Jesus bother to die?"

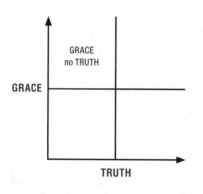

White says this has become the unofficial pop culture stance of our day. *Accept, tolerate, and affirm every behavior, or be labeled a hatemonger.* To refuse to affirm all behavior is labeled as condemning and intolerant. But if you affirm all behavior, you're actually not full of grace at all, because there's no need for such things in your world. You're wanting God's blessing, while at the same time rejecting God himself. You are left without any solutions to the problems of injustice, evil, and rebellion. In fact, those words should not even be part of your vocabulary, because your position demands you affirm even the most heinous of crimes.

People come to such thinking for good and bad reasons. Many

possess a genuine concern for others, so their worldview goes like this: "Because I love people, I will speak against no one." The problem is that no one can carry this out logically or philosophically. If you witnessed a man violently abusing a child, you are forced to choose sides, immediately. To remain silent would be to hate the child. Even those with genuine, good reasons for a "grace but no truth" worldview end up in a place of hate.

Darker intentions also lead to this worldview. Paul warned Timothy,

Instead, to suit their own desires, they will gather around them a great number of teachers to say what their itching ears want to hear. They will turn their ears away from the truth and turn aside to myths.

2 TIMOTHY 4:3-4

I had the privilege of working with teenagers for sixteen years. I wasn't alarmed when one of them, a young man named Javon, told me he wasn't sure if he believed in God. I'd heard it many times, and I knew it could mean many things. Maybe Javon was going through the natural, healthy process of thinking through his faith apart from his parents, or maybe he'd been dumped by his girlfriend and was just mad. As it turned out, an ignoble, yet common, pattern of events was at play. Javon was sleeping with his girlfriend and experimenting with drugs and alcohol. He knew these things were wrong and unhealthy, but long-term plans weren't on his mind. Guilt became a huge problem for him. How could he reconcile his faith and his actions? He chose what many have chosen before him—he modified his faith.

To gloss over the difficult teachings of Jesus is to gloss over Jesus himself. If Jesus really is the Truth, if he really died and rose again, then we must resist any temptation to misshape his words in order to cram them into our worldview. Instead, we must align our lives with his words. The message of Christ is for *all* people, but those *all* people must come to Christ on *all* his terms.

If a mob dragged a racist before Jesus, ready to string him up, Jesus might say, "Let he who is without sin take this man to the gallows." The mob would drop the rope, and Jesus might say to the man, "Neither do I condemn you." But while freeing him of the noose, would Jesus say, "Now go, carry on"? Of course not! He'd tell the man to repent of his sinful ways. He might put a firm hand on the man's shoulder and say, "When you despise others, you despise me. Do *not* do it again."

When a friend shares about an area of ongoing sin and struggle, don't cut the story short. If a warning needs to follow a hug, give it. I like people to feel forgiven and happy, so sometimes I gloss over the truth they need to hear. If I care for them, I must also include words of truth.

I'm thankful for friends who, after showering me with grace, tacked on some truth such as "You are busy, so don't neglect your family," and "Church leadership feels complex; don't forget the simple command to make disciples."

We don't do God any favors by watering down his demands. We must tell the whole story, truth and all.

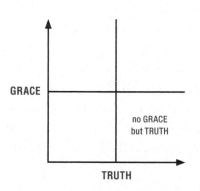

Option 3 indulges in the worst of legalism and fundamentalism. There are rules and regulations, dos and don'ts, laws and legalities, but no grace. After all, truth hurts, right? Of all the worldviews, it builds the deepest, most violent, and most dangerous bunkers.

Welcome to Islam, moralism, saved-by-works theology, and fundamentalism—even fundamentalist Christianity—where people cower in uncertainty, fear, and despair. The freeing lightness of grace eludes them.

When people try to walk in truth detached from grace, they leave behind a trail of wounded, condemned victims in need of rescue. Some of you reading this paragraph are still limping around due to the wounds caused by people pursuing *truth at all costs*. Some of you might even still be wounding others, because you've believed the lie that God cares more about truth than love.

I pray those in this bunker will accept the jarring reality that the God of all truth is also the God of all grace—so to walk without grace is to miss out on the truest thing in the universe. Some people claim to defend truth, but they only defend the components of truth nestled underneath the banner of morality, and they are pretty selective in which moral laws deserve our attention. They completely dismiss God's commands of love, gentleness, and compassion.

A few years ago, a man started showing up at our church on Sundays. To say he disliked my preaching would be a monumental understatement. He wrote me the most mean-spirited letter I've ever received. I asked him to meet with me, and he said, "Really? I'd be glad to talk. I've never had a preacher meet with me after I sent a letter." Aha. One of those guys.

When we got together for coffee, he cheerfully greeted me and even listened to me explain how terribly inaccurate his accusations were. I highlighted his claims with actual statements from my manuscript (color-coded, of course), and he backed off his attack. A few weeks later, he even invited me to a parade. Well, to be specific, he invited me to go with him to protest a gay-rights parade. I declined.

A few days later, my heart sank when I saw his picture in the newspaper. There he was, standing on a street with a sign that said something like "God hates sinners." You want to know how that sign read to the people in the parade? "God hates you." He was in his bunker, inviting me to join him, and at the same time driving his victims into opposite bunkers.

Our church leaders wanted zero association with his actions. I told him we wouldn't tolerate his behavior, so he chose to *bless* another church with his presence.

Too often, in a world full of brokenness and anger, we allow segments of truth to become an idol rather than looking to the one who is the fullness of Truth. Of course, most people aren't as mean as the letter-writing, parade-protesting guy. Many people project a lack of grace because they obsess about the slice of truth that dominates their attention. They rightfully lament wrongs in this world, but they wrongly elevate their lament above all others. These lamenters can be well-intentioned—but I find myself bruised nonetheless. I'd like to share some of my personal experiences, but you have to promise not to pity me or think I'm whining. It's not the biggest deal in the world, but I think it will help you understand how our obsession about one slice of truth can project a lack of grace and kindness.

I love feedback and deep discussions, but we all know the difference between a genuine question and a passive-aggressive dig. Last year a person pulled me aside and asked me to speak out more against child abuse. Another chided me for not saying more about marriage issues. Another slipped me printouts about political corruption (leaving out the corruption found in their own political party). Another asked why I said so much about a racially divisive event in our town, and another stated that those who didn't address it more were contributing to the divisiveness.

I needed a nap.

I love these people, and I share in their sorrow and anger. I speak against these symptoms of brokenness. I advocate, write, pray, give, volunteer, and serve on a board. Many people are thankful for this, but for others, it's never enough. They're never satisfied. Their issues dominate them. I fear they wish more for the demise of their opponents than for their redemption. (Has their lament become their god? Have my laments become my gods? Do you need a nap after we talk?)

If we pursue truth without grace, we'll wind up with neither.

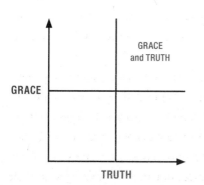

Only one approach will help us dance in no man's land. Authentic Christianity brings together both truth and grace, which were intertwined in the life of Jesus. White labeled John 1:14, which describes Jesus as "full of grace and truth," as a theological bombshell. One man embodied grace. One man embodied truth. One man. One God.

Grace and truth found their perfect union in Christ, but the rest of us tend to gravitate toward one or the other. Truth without grace breeds self-righteousness and legalism. Grace without truth breeds deception and moral compromise. The key to true Christian spirituality is to integrate these two qualities into life, imitating the character of Christ.[5]

We need grace because we're condemned to hell without it. We need truth because we're condemned to hell without it. We need both, because grace and truth let us see the true God, grace and truth light our path, grace and truth free us from shame, and grace and truth lead us to eternity.

My friend Caleb Kaltenbach grew up with a father and mother who both came out as gay, then divorced when he was young. They abhorred his decision as a teenager to follow Christ. Caleb learned that life would require messy grace.[6] How could he love God, the Bible, his church, and his parents at the same time? He committed to try, for to love God requires us to love all people. The love of God spread through him to many around him.

"Love," he often says, "is the tension between grace and truth." It will be messy, because people are messy. Our problems, struggles, and relationships are messy. So we must embrace the tension in order to love. And love is what we shall do.

CHICKEN WARS

When news broke in 2012 that Dan Cathy, then president of fast-food giant Chick-fil-A, opposed gay marriage, America wouldn't have noticed if aliens invaded. Special-interest groups bunkered down and students boycotted. Supporters flocked to support Chick-fil-A, while detractors waved their protest signs. And the media—oh, the media. I pictured news producers giggling like schoolgirls at the thought of a ratings bonanza. They shoved their microphones in the faces of anyone with a harsh opinion willing to talk. They left no chicken nugget unturned.

The whole fiasco depressed me. I saw friends on both sides of the debate wound and get wounded. It seemed the entire country had joined one of two bunkers and was hurling verbal grenades at each other. Opinions shed even the thinnest layer of gentleness. Questions went unasked and dialogue went radio silent. Hate lit up the sky.

If you were heavily invested in this debate, the previous two paragraphs might have just ticked you off. You might be wondering how someone could remain neutral on such a divisive topic. I'd remind you that neutrality is not our goal. We're chasing love and truth. Creating peace in an altogether hostile environment is our goal. In the end, all of those sharp, harsh statements changed nobody's mind. The harsh words only drove people further from wisdom.

But quietly, even secretly, two people chose to leave their bunkers. When I first read the story, I shot out of my chair and raised my hands to the sky. It had happened! It had finally happened! Thank you, God, for such an example.

In a *Huffington Post* article, homosexual advocate Shane Windmeyer "came out" that he'd befriended Dan Cathy. People were shell-shocked that the leader of Campus Pride would go from leading boycotts against Chick-fil-A to calling its leader a friend.[7] Windmeyer's article explains how their unlikely friendship came to be:

> In the heat of the controversy, I got a surprise call from Dan Cathy. . . . I took the call with great caution. He was going to tear me apart, right? . . . Turn his lawyers on me?
>
> The first call lasted over an hour, and the private conversation led to more calls the next week and the week after. . . .
>
> His questions and a series of deeper conversations ultimately led to a number of in-person meetings. . . . He had never before had such dialogue with any member of the LGBT community. It was awkward at times but always genuine and kind.
>
> It is not often that people with deeply held and completely opposing viewpoints actually risk sitting down and listening to

one another. . . . Dan Cathy and I would, together, try to do better than each of us had experienced before. . . .

Dan sought first to understand, not to be understood. He confessed that he had been naïve to the issues at hand and the unintended impact of his company's actions. . . .

Through all this, Dan and I shared respectful, enduring communication and built trust. His demeanor has always been one of kindness and openness. Even when I continued to directly question his public actions and the funding decisions, Dan embraced the opportunity to have dialogue and hear my perspective. He and I were committed to a better understanding of one another. Our mutual hope was to find common ground if possible, and to build respect no matter what. . . .

We were each entirely ourselves. . . . Neither of us could— or would—change. It was not possible. We were different but in dialogue. That was progress.

Both leaders took a chance. I'd like to think that their effort toward healthy dialogue would be universally applauded, but that has not been the case. Windmeyer took a beating from those who used to call him friend. They labeled him *traitor* and *sellout*. Cathy has also opened himself to fresh criticism. We can always expect that kind of crossfire in no man's land.

Like Windmeyer, I'd label their dialogue as one of progress. As a follower of Jesus, I'm thrilled Cathy grew in his understanding and compassion for a group of people from whom he'd been previously alienated. As a follower of Jesus, I'm also thrilled that Windmeyer learned about and saw Cathy's faith. I wonder when he last sat in the kind company of a Christian. Grace paved the way for learning. Learning paves the way for truth to be learned. Rule of thumb: grace first, then truth.

As a citizen of our country, I'm inspired by both men. I don't know either of them personally. Either might disappoint me tomorrow. But on this day, I stand and applaud two men who got out of their bunkers. Grace broke through. Now truth has a fighting chance.

LOVE

I struggle daily to embrace both grace and truth. I often feel myself leaning toward one at the expense of the other, forgetting that they *are not opposites* but are rather fraternal twins. I wonder how to confront sin with grace, and foolishness with truth. It feels like a dance.

I bet you feel this tension too. You've cloaked your speech in grace and been accused of riding a slippery slope to a watered-down gospel. You've cloaked your speech in truth and been accused of taking the Bible too literally. Sometimes you feel as if you can't win.

Yet it's good to speak graciously, even when we think someone holds dangerous, horrific ideas. It's good to speak truthfully, even when truth becomes unpopular. We just have to figure out how to speak with grace and truth, and we'll pursue this daunting task because that's what love demands. I'm convinced this struggle won't go away, so let's unpack our bags in no man's land, brace for resistance, and throw a party when others join us.

REFLECTION QUESTIONS

1. How did the Pharisees intend to trap Jesus in John 8?

2. Make a list of the different emotions and thoughts you think the woman had during her few minutes with Jesus.

3. Are there some "yes or no" questions that you need to start answering with more nuance, as Jesus did?

4. Which quadrants have you inhabited?

5. What did you learn from the story of Dan Cathy and Shane Windmeyer? Can you recall similar stories?

CHAPTER 8

WISDOM AND TACT

———

When Arioch, the commander of the king's guard, had gone out to put to death the wise men of Babylon, Daniel spoke to him with wisdom and tact.

DANIEL 2:14

ONE OF MY FAVORITE CHARACTERS from the Old Testament, and one of the people who inspired me to write this book, is Daniel. He found himself in a nearly impossible situation, one in which he'd have to compromise either truth or peace.

Daniel found himself as a captive and exile under the rule of the ancient Babylonian king Nebuchadnezzar. Words like *ruthless*, *spoiled*, and *volatile* describe Nebuchadnezzar well. *Brilliant* describes him too. His military and architectural achievements brought him fame, but his foolishness was never far away.

One night Nebuchadnezzar had a deeply disturbing dream.[1] He was so rattled that he summoned all of the magicians, enchanters, sorcerers, and astrologers—which truly was a great honor. It's not every day the most powerful man in the world calls you to solve his problems.

Their good feelings would soon turn into a nightmare.

Nebuchadnezzar proclaimed, "This is what I have firmly decided: If you do not tell me what my dream was and interpret it, I will have you cut into pieces and your houses turned into piles of rubble."[2]

They were prepared to tell him *what the dream meant*, but nobody expected him to order them to tell him *what he dreamed*. They tried to trick the king by saying things like "Okay. No problem. Just go ahead and tell us your dream, and then we will interpret it."

Nebuchadnezzar wasn't budging. He demanded they tell him *what* he dreamed first. "If you do not," he said, "there is only one penalty."[3]

They answered him with charges of unfairness, complaining that no man on earth could meet his demand. Stumbling onto some truth, they admitted that only a god could know what the king had dreamed.

And so Nebuchadnezzar ordered their execution, along with every wise man in the land—and that included Daniel.

Daniel had been enslaved by King Nebuchadnezzar. He'd survived the siege and collapse of Judah and the Israelite trail of tears, being marched away from their homeland. He'd lost his country, home, belongings, and family, and then he was forced to serve the wicked king who'd caused his harm. Insult to injury.

Daniel had served Nebuchadnezzar well, but the inability of the other wise men to tell Nebuchadnezzar what he'd dreamed placed a kill order on him. And just when it looked like Daniel had nowhere to turn, he found no man's land.

When Arioch, the commander of the king's guard, had gone out to put to death the wise men of Babylon, Daniel spoke to him with wisdom and tact.

DANIEL 2:14

Daniel opted for a revolutionary peace plan. Notice what he did *not* do:

- panic
- act irrationally
- manipulate

- bribe
- lie
- run for cover
- berate the king
- form alliances
- organize a rebellion
- draw a sword

No, Daniel instead spoke with wisdom and tact. His words were measured and careful. His wisdom and tact prevented the slaughter of many innocent people. They saved families, preserved future generations, and allowed him to have a continued voice in the conversation. By speaking with wisdom and tact, Daniel stayed in step with God's will for his life. He overcame the trappings of bunker living. His wise and tactful response illuminated a trail scarcely traveled.

SERVING DINNER WITH TACT

Tact is "a keen sense of what to say or do to avoid giving offense; skill in dealing with difficult or delicate situations";[4] the ability to say and do what is tasteful.

In my younger and more immature days, I thought I could add some fun to a week of camp by rolling up chocolate brownies in the shape of dog doo-doo. I stacked them in a pile under a tree. (Did I mention how young and immature I was at that time?) When some junior high campers walked by, I dared them to take a bite from the pile. They about got sick just thinking about it. When I picked one up and took a bite, they did get sick. These same campers would've given anything for an extra brownie earlier in the cafeteria. But now that I'd made the brownies appear so gross, they wouldn't touch them.

Trying to give wisdom without tact is like that. When I try to teach my kids a life lesson by using sarcasm, I'm serving them wisdom without tact. I may have all the right ingredients, but if the presentation is ugly, they will never take a bite.

But imagine you're out walking on a cold day. A friend welcomes you into her warm house. As you walk in, cheerful music is playing. You smell freshly baked bread—and there, waiting on the table for you, is a hot bowl of soup. How can you refuse it? In the same way, wisdom becomes a desirable thing in the welcoming warmth of tact.

Tact gives us an audience. It defuses anger and provides space for our voices to be heard. And in that space, we can offer wisdom.

A PLATE OF WISDOM

Wisdom is applied knowledge. You can know facts about how seat belts save lives, but if you don't buckle up, you lack wisdom. Wisdom goes below the surface of knowledge. It's tried, tested, and found to be trustworthy.

One time my college roommates and I decided to make a meal for our friends. We cleaned house, bought the ingredients, followed the instructions, and set the table. The salad was tasty, but then we took a bite of the chicken. It tasted like soap! We'd scrubbed the pan but neglected to rinse off the soap. The first bite was our last. We tossed the chicken and ordered pizza.

Tact without wisdom is like serving something that looks delicious until you take a bite. If your friend wants to know what you think about his buying a $30,000 car with his $25,000 salary, he needs more than smiling reassurance. He needs you to read Proverbs 22:7 to him: "The borrower is slave to the lender." Don't willingly watch him become a slave to the car dealership for the next decade. Otherwise, you've served him a plate of delicious-looking soap.

What if wisdom were highly valued in our world? What if wisdom were taught, modeled, and grasped? What if marriages, businesses, and Washington, DC, (gasp) hungered for wisdom?

No man's land is a place of wisdom. Any fool can hunker in a bunker. The wise find ways out.

Wisdom begins with God. He created us, he knows what is best for us, and he graciously gives wisdom to us. James 1:5 says, "If any of you lacks wisdom, you should ask God, who gives generously to all without finding fault, and it will be given to you." God has given our world an amazing resource, the Bible. I hope you'll develop a ravenous appetite for it.

THE FOUR WAYS OF WISDOM AND TACT

Daniel's counterintuitive response to Nebuchadnezzar reveals why it's critical to speak with wisdom and tact. Without tact, wisdom cannot be heard. Without wisdom, tact only makes foolishness more palatable. But when wisdom and tact are paired, you can apply knowledge that welcomes people to hear it, and you can dance in no man's land, even when your life is on the line. *Especially* when your life is on the line.

As Daniel's story unfolds, we learn four profound yet doable principles of wisdom and tact. Daniel . . .

1. Asked questions
2. Showed restraint
3. Prayed
4. Obeyed

// 1. QUESTIONS

[Daniel] asked the king's officer, "Why did the king issue such a harsh decree?" Arioch then explained the matter to Daniel. At this, Daniel went in to the king and asked for time, so that he might interpret the dream for him.

DANIEL 2:15-16

Three times in the first two chapters, Daniel responded to a crisis with a question.[5] When Arioch broke the bad news, Daniel responded with a sincere, calm question. And it worked. Arioch granted him a hearing with the king.

How I wish that I could go back in time to replace accusations with thoughtful questions. One of those times would be with my friend Karl. Karl serves our church with excellence and joy. I've loved partnering with such a good friend on numerous projects. A few years ago I sat down with him to share my concerns regarding how he handled an incident. I'd heard about it from a couple of people but failed to learn from one key person: Karl. I should have predicted the results of confronting him in my ignorance.

What could've been resolved with a few questions resulted in hurt feelings, two follow-up meetings, apologies from me, and egg on my face. Some of my biggest leadership blunders have happened because I either corrected or accused before asking questions.

This blunder creeps into other areas of my life too. I've too often blurted correction before asking a thoughtful question to my wife, my children, or the kids in the baseball dugout. I've been guilty of digging into a fight, as opposed to digging into the matter in a search for truth.

The next time a crisis erupts in your house or in the headlines, test yourself. Are you digging in for a fight? Are you digging for truth and suspending judgment? What are those around you doing? Are you offering death or life . . . digging graves or wells?

// 2. RESTRAINT

Daniel's questions reflect a calmness rarely seen in times of crisis. Time was running out, yet he did not act or speak rashly. He didn't lash out or yield control to some emotional flare-up. Instead, he showed self-control.

Uncontrolled, unfiltered words and actions trigger family feuds and global crises. God lovingly gave us emotions, but he also gave us the ability to manage our words and actions. Wise people place an hourglass between the *action done to them* and the *reaction cast forth from them*:

Action Reaction

Sometimes our hourglasses run too short. When something hurtful is done to us, we need to let some time and raw emotions pass. This gives us opportunity to filter out the hurtful things we would say and do if we still lived in a bunker.

Sometimes our hourglasses go too long. In other words, we avoid any and all confrontation. Every healthy, deep relationship requires some corrective face-to-face chats. Small, healthy confrontations prevent big explosions, which happen when we bottle up wounds and frustrations for months and years at a time.

The wife of my friend Esteban used to bemoan his hot temper. She stuffed her emotions and honesty inside, afraid the bomb in him would detonate. Eventually, she couldn't live on eggshells anymore. She wisely sought the advice of church leaders and developed a plan full of wisdom and tact. She could've run away, she could've fought back, or she could've tried to ignore his sin, but instead she chose the courageous path. After some excruciating months, progress began to be made in their relationship. Now a decade removed from the crisis, she knows the safe love of her husband. She finds sweet shelter in his gentleness. Time didn't change him; Jesus did. But his wife played a crucial role. I watched him confess his sin and allow God's grace and Spirit to do the work in him. God can do this work in you, too.

// 3. PRAYER

> Daniel returned to his house and explained the matter to his friends. . . . He urged them to plead for mercy from the God of heaven.
>
> DANIEL 2:17-18

Daniel's unrelenting prayer life guarded his heart against any sort of bunker mentality. The Lord helped him discern what to say and how to say it. Daniel walked with God, and God walked with Daniel. His prayer life both built and revealed his character:

1. *He chose prayer over panic* (Daniel 2:18). I panic when I rely on myself or some other mere mortal. But I remain calm when I rely on divine power. Prayers guard our hearts against the bunker mentality of panic.

2. *He gave thanks* (Daniel 2:20; 6:10). Has God ever answered your prayer, yet you forgot to thank him? Yep, me too. Daniel's thankful recognition of God reveals that he was dependent upon him in the bad times and the good. He took nothing for granted, so every good gift was a blessing from God. Prayers guard our hearts against the bunker mentality of entitlement.

3. *He was disciplined in his prayers* (Daniel 6:10). Out of fear of legalism, many run far from disciplined habits. Others may use this as a convenient excuse, but a lack of discipline reflects a lack of commitment (in finances, football, poetry, and prayer). Three times a day, Daniel opened his windows, got on his knees, and prayed. I believe his discipline in prayer gave him focus and joy in no man's land, even with people conspiring against him. Prayers guard our hearts against the bunker mentality of laziness.

4. *He confessed* (Daniel 9:4-19). He was not the one rebelling against God, but you would never know it by his confessional prayers. He owned the sins of the people, and he pleaded with God for forgiveness.

   The proud man bristles when asked to apologize for something that he did not directly do: *"It wasn't my fault you were wounded. Get over it."* Or *"I can't help that my dog tore up your flower bed."* Or *"It's a habit I inherited from my dad."* Prayers guard our hearts against the bunker mentality of avoidance.

5. *He humbled himself* (Daniel 9:18). Daniel depended upon God rather than his own power. He prayed, "We do not make requests of you because we are righteous, but because of your great mercy." We often act as if God owes us something. God owes us nothing, for all is grace. Prayers guard our hearts against the bunker mentality of arrogance.

   Daniel knew God held no obligation to listen, but God still turned his ear toward him. God listened because God is good.

But the text also says God listened because Daniel was "highly esteemed" (Daniel 9:23). Daniel's reputation preceded him, even in heaven. God answered him before the prayer even left his lips.

> Since the first day that you set your mind to gain understanding and to humble yourself before your God, your words were heard, and I have come in response to them.
>
> DANIEL 10:12

The moment Daniel recognized his unworthiness of God's response, God responded. When we care about others, when we seek to learn rather than to teach, when we prostrate ourselves as modest rather than proud—when we humble ourselves—we catch God's attention.

We've established how counterintuitive and difficult no man's land can be, but I hope you're catching how beautiful it can also be. Whether you're in a bunker or in no man's land, trials will come your way. Imagine if you face those challenges with the Spirit of Christ, as Daniel did. Don't you want to be a person of prayer: calm, grateful, disciplined, responsible, and humble?

// 4. OBEDIENCE

The temptation to attempt to control the outcomes of situations can chain us like slaves. When we're locked in on outcomes, obedience disappears from our minds. But obedience is wisdom. Daniel chose obedience, focusing on following God in the face of death rather than trying to scheme against Babylon, the evil empire.

Daniel's friends Shadrach, Meshach, and Abednego[6] also chose obedience. They were given a simple choice: "Worship this idol or be burned to death." They staked their ground: "If we are thrown into the blazing furnace, the God we serve is able to deliver us from it. . . . But even if he does not, we want you to know, Your Majesty, that we will not serve your gods or worship the image of gold you have set up."[7] Choosing obedience, they left the outcome to God. And don't miss how they spoke with both wisdom and tact, holding truth and peace together. They proved faithful to God and still made it known that they were at peace with their oppressor, even as they were thrown to their assumed death. (Spoiler alert: They didn't die.)

Later in the book, Daniel chose death-by-lions over spurning his God. Through obedience he abdicated all outcomes to God's hands.[8]

I've had to learn this hard lesson myself. In December of 2006, on a van ride home from a ski conference in Colorado, my wife started a conversation that forever changed my life:

"I think God wants us to adopt internationally."

"Wow! Okay," I said. "Let's pray about it for a while."

So we prayed. And then we prayed some more.

By the fall of 2007, we were ready to take the plunge. We took classes and chose an adoption agency based in Southeast Asia. But when their government heaped additional regulations upon orphanages, our agency was nearly crippled. The agency kindly encouraged us to look elsewhere. It was a setback, but we are still thankful for their honesty.

After times of prayer and learning, our eyes turned toward Ethiopia. Beth was old enough (many countries require the parents to be over a certain age), I had spent some time in Africa, our family supported an African child through Compassion International, and our schedule and budget could survive Ethiopia's adoption requirements.

So in March of 2008, we began completing the stacks of paperwork required to adopt from Ethiopia. We finished in September. There's a reason they call it *the paper pregnancy*. The costs and discomforts grow by the month.

The sweetest moment in the process occurred when our family had to get blood work done. On the way out of the medical office, one of our boys asked, "So, can we have our sister now?" We wished it were that simple.

The waiting began . . .

In March of 2009, we were still waiting, but we were also talking. During her morning devotions, Beth kept feeling that God wanted us to consider adopting two children. So we prayed about opening our adoption status to include siblings.

But before we could change our status on the adoption, we got *the call*. Few words can describe the joy of that moment. We heard that a daughter was coming to our family, read her name, saw her picture, and pored over her bio. Breathtaking. Ultrasounds are cool, but they can't compete with a real picture of a little girl, ready for you to bring her home.

In one instant, we knew our daughter's name, face, and story. We fell in love. By the end of the week, we felt as if we had loved her our whole lives. She graced my dreams nightly.

But then, pain.

Just five days after *the call*, Beth told me to sit down. We were pregnant.

I laughed out loud and said, "What in the world?" But after about five seconds of shock and amusement, my emotions changed. The question loomed: "Does this derail our adoption?" The adoption agency's policy states that if an adopting couple gets pregnant during the process, the adoption is put on hold.[9] I can't tell you the heartache I experienced. Someone was going to take my child.

In between tears, I frantically searched the Internet for help. I read stories of about fifty couples who had gone through similar situations, and all of them recommended we keep it a secret. If we could keep the pregnancy hidden from the adoption agency, we could still adopt our child.

Up next: the search for a biblical reason to deceive. That's a tough thing to find.

In the middle of the night, I gazed out the bedroom window intended for our daughter. As the clouds crawled under the moon, questions crawled through my heart: *Will I take her picture down in my office? How long will this hurt? Will she find another home? Why us?*

The darkness gave no ground to morning sunshine. I left my office by 9:00, because I could not control the tears.

Some close friends met me for lunch, and I shared my dilemma. Should I hide our secret or be honest with our adoption agency? That's when Kenneth, a longtime friend, said exactly what I needed to hear: "You know what's right. You've never been in control of this whole thing anyway. God has been and still is. Your honesty with the adoption agency will not change that."

I went home early and prepared to make the most nerve-racking call of my life. I penned an eloquent plea, rehearsed it, and dialed the number. I found myself relenting to honesty and faith, but also preparing to call back every day for weeks if denied. I would do anything, but *anything* would probably be insufficient. Obedience, rather than outcome, started to drive my faith. That's all faith is: obedience regardless of outcome.

The lady from the agency concluded our conversation by saying, "Thank you for being honest. It's a case-by-case decision and will involve my directors. Don't lose all hope."

Follow-up work dominated the next few days, as they sought to determine whether we were fit to adopt and birth a child within a matter of months. We painstakingly crafted answers to their e-mail questions, garnered additional references, and tried to keep our voices confident during phone interviews.

Then the waiting began again.

After a few more days, we received official word that everything was a go. Joy, relief, and gratitude consumed us. It's a story I'll never forget. Looking back, I would not trade the pain, tears, or stress.

This story is not about us at all. It's about God. He was gracious to us. Through the waiting and uncertainty, God taught us to focus on obedience, not outcomes.

Do you trust God to take care of the outcomes, or do you pretend as if you control such things? Bunker dwellers try to control. Those in no man's land trust and obey. What is keeping you from obedience?

THE REST OF THE STORY

After Daniel responded with wisdom and tact to Arioch, Nebuchadnezzar's henchman, God revealed the dream and its interpretation to Daniel during the night. His confidence convinced Arioch, because Arioch introduced him to the king as "a man . . . who can tell the king what his dream means" (Daniel 2:25). Daniel delivered.

"Only God could reveal your dream," Daniel told Nebuchadnezzar. "You dreamed of a large statue—an enormous, dazzling statue, awesome in appearance and consisting of gold, silver, bronze, iron, and clay. But it won't stand forever. It will be crushed, bit by bit. The rock that topples it will eventually become a mountain and fill the whole earth."[10]

King Nebuchadnezzar's eyes must've widened. Daniel vividly narrated the king's dream. If someone can tell you your dream, they've earned the right to interpret it.

"God has given you dominion and power and glory," Daniel revealed to him. "After you, another kingdom will arise, inferior to yours. Next, a third and fourth kingdom will rise and fall. But finally, God will set up a kingdom that will never be destroyed."[11]

Nebuchadnezzar fell prostrate before Daniel, confessing that his God was the God of gods.

Instead of executing Daniel and his friends, he promoted them.

Nebuchadnezzar, sadly, returned to foolishness. But Daniel remained faithful.

Daniel never dived into a bunker. Ever.[12] He never viewed Nebuchadnezzar as the enemy. Soak that in: Daniel did not view the man wanting to kill him *as an enemy*. And yet, he also never violated his faith. He knew he waged war not against flesh and blood, but against the principalities and powers. In the midst of an oppressive regime, Daniel demonstrated Jesus' statement "Give back to Caesar what is Caesar's, and to God what is God's."[13] (We'll delve into that story later. Stay tuned.)

The past month our country has weathered a hurricane, deadly wild-fires, and a horrific mass shooting. Shockingly, none of these stories has dominated the headlines as much as a nationwide argument about the national anthem. Here's a two-minute version from my perspective:

A couple of dozen NFL players were kneeling during the national anthem in order to draw attention to racial inequalities. Kneeling was first suggested by a former Green Beret, who felt that it would be perceived as respectful, as opposed to sitting. However, many people were offended, feeling that the mode of protest was disrespectful to our military, flag, and country. The story had been simmering for a year, but when the president said the protesting players should be fired, it hit fever pitch. That Sunday, almost two hundred players knelt during the playing of the anthem. By Sunday night, everyone, including hordes of politicans, had an opinion—and they were eager to share it. A month later, the media is still milking it for all it's worth.

I tried to remove myself from the specific argument and just look at it from a distance. I had good Christian friends on both side of the argument, and I grieved at the sight of the church being divided over the issue. When that happens, Satan wins every time. As long as we're hating each other from our bunkers, he could care less who wins the actual argument.

The one thing I didn't find much was a combination of wisdom and tact. But then I read an article written by Nate Boyer, the former Green Beret who'd suggested kneeling as a respectful protest. Boyer was well positioned to speak out. He had skin in the game with both sides, and his diverse friendships gave him a broad perspective. You could tell he was grieved, and then he offered an amazing, no man's land idea: The president and the player who first knelt should meet and talk. They should help us heal and get better. He wrote,

It seems like we just hate each other; and that is far more painful to me than any protest, or demonstration, or rally, or tweet. We're told to pick a side, there's a line drawn in the sand "are you with us or against us?" . . .

I believe that progress and real change happens in this world when you reach across the divide, you build a bridge, you swallow your pride, you open your mind, you embrace what you don't understand, and ultimately you surrender. . . .

So I'll be here, standing in the radical middle, doing what I can to continue fighting for those that can't fight for themselves. Let's get this thing fixed together, you and me. I love you all with all my heart.[14]

The meeting hasn't happened, but it got me to wondering. Imagine what it would be like to live in a world with wisdom and tact:

Friendships would grow deeper and last for life. Every one of them.

Families would stay together.

Neighbors would be neighborly.

Cities would be harmonious.

Countries would be peaceful.

Next time that you are in a hot spot, remember Daniel. He honored God, persuaded a king, and saved the day by speaking with wisdom and tact.

PRAYER EXERCISE

We gave lots of attention in this chapter to the importance of prayer. But I never like to just talk or write about prayer without inviting us to actually do it. Is now an appropriate time for you to stop and pray? Do you recognize areas in your life in which you've set aside wisdom and tact in favor of harsh reactions or foolish arguments? Allow me to offer a few suggestions as you seek to step into no man's land through prayer:

- Confess the sins of those in your community. The fighting of your people grieves the Father.

    The following prayer is molded from Ezra 9 and 10, which speaks of communal guilt, bitter weeping, fasting, and prayer:

    "What has happened to us is a result of our evil deeds and our great guilt, and yet, our God, you have punished us less than our sins deserved" (Ezra 9:13). "Here we are before you in our guilt, though because of it not one of us can stand in your presence" (Ezra 9:15).

    We are guilty of pride. We've turned a blind eye to your commands. We've prompted hate. We've caused divides. The weight of our sin weighs heavy on us. Forgive us, Lord. We commit to your ways. Your will be done.

- Confess your own sins and plea for a renewed spirit. Recognize where you've dug into a bunker instead of digging for the truth.

Ask for wisdom and tact when you are worn down by the battles waging around you. The following prayer is molded from Psalm 51:

Create in me a clean heart, O God. It's filthy right now. I've been more concerned about proving myself right than I have been about being righteous. I'm scared to death that you'll leave me. I can't live without you, and I believe your promise of forgiveness. So forgive me, Lord. Let me feel what it's like to have a clean soul. Let me be clean. And I promise to teach others your ways. Thank you, thank you, thank you, God, for second chances. I commit to pursuing the wisdom and tact you've taught me from the book of Daniel and showed me through your Son.

REFLECTION QUESTIONS

1. What do you think it was like for Daniel to serve Nebuchadnezzar?

2. Are you more apt to proceed without wisdom or tact?

3. Which of the principles that helped Daniel live with wisdom and tact most needs your focus? Do you need to ask questions, show restraint, pray, or obey—or do several of those things together?

4. Is there an area of your life in which you need to quit worrying about the outcome and just obey? What will that look like?

5. Please take some time with the prayer exercise today. Please don't skip it.

CHAPTER 9

GENTLENESS AND STRENGTH

Through patience a ruler can be persuaded, and a gentle tongue can break a bone.

PROVERBS 25:15

IN GALATIANS 5, among a host of heavyweight virtues—love, joy, peace, patience, kindness—we find one that might deserve the title *Most Overlooked*. I can't recall hearing a sermon about it. Authors don't write about it. Some people dismiss it as nothing but a personality trait. And others even take pride in their lack of it, making fun of others who embody it. But no matter how much we might dismiss it, few virtues hold more power than gentleness.

Other Bible books join Galatians' fruit of the Spirit list in trumpeting gentleness. Paul says we are to be clothed in it (Colossians 3:12). Proverbs speaks of its power (25:15). Daniel, Esther, Moses, Hosea, Isaac, Joseph, and others demonstrate it. The Lord speaks to us with gentleness (1 Kings 19:12). Jesus uses it to describe himself (Matthew 11:29) and perfectly modeled it.

Never make the mistake of mislabeling strength as brutal or gentleness as weak. Gentleness is strength transformed into control. Plato used the word *gentle* to describe a formerly wild but now-tamed beast.[1] In Greek literature the word also describes powerful horses standing calmly together, ready for service. Gentleness is not the absence of strength; it's the harnessing of it.

USEFULNESS

Deep in the heart of Texas, Beth and I rose before the sun and stumbled to the stables of the camp where we'd taken our family for vacation. A dozen other sleepy souls shuffled our way, ready for the morning trail ride.

I expected to be greeted with a southern "howdy," but everyone was quiet, including the ranch hands. I passed the awkward hush by retying my shoes.

A look of disgust wrinkled the tan face of Swanee, the head wrangler. While holding the reins of a beautiful horse, he broke the morning silence: "Sometimes he just wants to do his own thing. He's one of my best, but he darn near killed me this morning. I could've really been hurt. Even a tame horse can revert to its old, reckless ways. He's a powerful horse, but today he's useless, even dangerous. It got me thinking—I wonder how often I sadden God by bucking against his will for my life."

Swanee mounted another horse and continued in his hushed tone, "The gentler a horse becomes, the more it listens to my whispers and senses my needs, the more I can unleash its strength in a positive direction. I don't even have to move the reins for this horse to go where I want her to go. I only have to look. She can sense where I'm looking. God wants to lead us like that. It's how you should want to lead others too."

Swanee then looked to the left, only slightly shifting his weight. His horse gently turned and followed his gaze. Swanee then looked to the right, and his horse stepped toward his gaze. The sleepiness in our eyes gave way to wonder.

A stiff-necked horse ignores words; it needs a strong hand. An obedient, gentle horse only needs a whisper. As it relinquishes its will, its strength becomes useful.

Gentleness turns raw power into useful strength. Likewise, you please God when his whispers propel you to act. A gentle Christian is a useful, joy-creating Christian.

I first met my friend Doug at an orphanage in Mexico. He played tag with kids, hauled concrete bricks to a house, and taught Bible lessons under a tree. The children flocked to him. Later that week, I spent a Sunday under a bridge with him. He took his church here once a month to set up a lunch buffet for a large homeless community. At this point in the story, you probably have a picture in your head of the kind of person Doug is, a gentle soul. I was surprised to later learn more about Doug. He holds two master's degrees and a PhD in philosophy. Enrollment in the philosophy class he taught quickly maxed out because his reputation as a professor was widely known at the University of Texas at San Antonio.

Doug could've used his intellectual and academic strength for his own gain, joining a bunker of wealthy elites. But instead, he submitted it to the will of Jesus. This made Doug highly useful and effective in the Kingdom. Doug's gentleness reminds me of Jesus.

OUR GENTLE KING

Only two people in Scripture are labeled as gentle: Moses and Jesus.[2] As I wrestled with this idea of gentleness and strength balanced together, and how these two things can enable us to navigate the most difficult situations we might face, I knew that the life of Jesus would hold the perspective I needed. Because no one carried the strength of gentleness like Jesus Christ.

When Jesus entered the scene, people felt beaten down by rules. They just couldn't keep up with all of the regulations the religious leaders kept loading on their backs. Righteousness, it seemed, could never be attained. So imagine their delight at Jesus' words:

> Take my yoke upon you and learn from me, for I am gentle
> and humble in heart, and you will find rest for your souls.
> MATTHEW 11:29

The Gentle King is a good king. He doesn't heap oppressive rules upon his people; he offers them true freedom. A good king gives a good law to his people, and he shows the people how to live.

Jesus liked the metaphor of the shepherd and sheep. Sheep lack fast legs, powerful jaws, and cunning minds, so they need protection. Jesus told how a hired hand would run for safety if he saw wolves coming. Not Jesus. He said, "I am the good shepherd. The good shepherd lays down his life for the sheep" (John 10:11). In case you were wondering, you are one of the sheep, and Jesus, your Good Shepherd, gave his life for you.

Jesus didn't just describe himself as gentle—he reached out in gentleness over and over again. When his good friend Lazarus died, Jesus went to the town of Bethany. Mary, the sister of Lazarus, met Jesus with tears pouring out of her eyes. And the shortest verse in the Bible says, "Jesus wept."[3] Jesus knew he had the strength to raise Lazarus from the dead, and that's exactly what he soon did, yet he still wept.

After seeing Jesus heal a blind man and then teach about the Good Shepherd, some of the Jews accused Jesus of being demon possessed. They acknowledged his power but attributed it to Satan.

Others said, "These are not the sayings of a man possessed by a demon. Can a demon open the eyes of the blind?" (John 10:21).

The contrasts between Jesus and a demon-possessed man are many, but two stand out in this case: First, demons brought destruction; Jesus brought restoration. Second, demons never cared about a blind guy. Jesus, on the other hand, seemed to truly care about all sorts of people. He even cared about the outcasts.

In Matthew 21:5, Matthew describes a gentle king riding a donkey into Jerusalem. We call this the Triumphal Entry. Jesus was and is the King. Colossians 1 reveals how he holds the whole cosmos together. Yet even on his journey into Jerusalem, he was described as gentle. He submitted his power and authority for good—for you, for me, and for the founding of a new society. Gentleness found itself draped over Jesus like a robe.

Imagine the strength it took to go to the cross. Even while being tortured to death, Jesus prayed, "Father, forgive them" (Luke 23:34). To the thief next to him he said, "Today you will be with me in paradise" (Luke 23:43). And he secured the care of his mother by telling his best friend, "Here is your mother" (John 19:27). The Cross spotlights the greatest act of combined strength and gentleness the world has ever seen. Jesus had the power to get his revenge, but he exercised the strength to endure the pain. He had enough breath to curse, but enough gentleness to instead offer grace. He is our Gentle King.

THE ENEMIES OF GENTLE STRENGTH

As much as we're drawn to the gentleness of others, few of us are inclined to be gentle. Outside forces pull us toward harshness. How many men believe real manhood stomps on the weak in order to get ahead? Machismo doesn't have the time or patience for gentleness. How many women believe real womanhood requires them to punch first just so they'll have a shot at equality? Harsh feminism sees gentleness as a liability.

We're pulled into bunkers by outside influences, but the more menacing obstacles between us and gentleness are found deep within our hearts. Enemies like selfishness, insensitivity, and laziness war against the call and command to be gentle in our engagement with others.

// SELFISHNESS

Turn my heart toward your statutes and not toward **selfish** gain.
PSALM 119:36, EMPHASIS MINE

On April 15, 1912, as the *Titanic* plummeted below the icy Atlantic waters, Lifeboat No. 1 sped toward safety. Its occupants had escaped the shipwreck that claimed the lives of more than fifteen hundred people. After three hours at sea, they were picked up by a larger vessel and then taken to New York City. When they set foot on land, not everyone celebrated their escape from death. One sickening truth emerged: Lifeboat No. 1 had twelve occupants, but it had room for forty. Accounts vary about what transpired before and during their escape, but we know they chose to not go back to rescue more people. At least twenty-eight more people could've been saved. Instead, the people on the boat did what we're all inclined to do: They thought of themselves.

Selfishness stands in direct opposition to the Golden Rule. Instead of doing to others as you would wish them to do to you, the selfish person considers his or her own wants first and foremost. The selfish person only helps when it's easy, convenient, safe, or beneficial. James 3:16 says, "Where you have envy and selfish ambition, there you find disorder and every evil practice." Selfishness disorders our lives too.

Selfishness destroys gentleness.

Selfishness causes us to be dismayed at everyone else's imperfections.

Selfishness escalates problems and pushes people's buttons.

Selfishness uses harshness to kick others down.

And while selfishness destroys gentleness, Christ-rooted selflessness builds it.

// INSENSITIVITY

A gentle answer turns away wrath,
　　but a harsh word stirs up anger.

PROVERBS 15:1

An insensitive remark feels like dirt in the face. Insensitivity is a lack of caring, a lack of awareness, a lack of understanding that you never know all of what's happening in someone else's life. Insensitivity lacks both gentleness and strength because it's easy and impulsive. My friend Johanna knows this all too well.

When Jeff and Johanna began noticing that their teenage daughter wasn't quite herself, they figured it was no big deal. But as some strange symptoms persisted, they figured that they'd better get her to a doctor. Nothing could prepare them for the words they'd hear: "Your girl has cancer." Suddenly, their family entered what often felt like the valley of death. At times my friends felt swallowed by grief, uncertainty, and weariness.

During one week that included chemotherapy and a late-night trip to the hospital, my friend still needed to shop for groceries. You still have to eat, even when the pain makes it hard to breathe. She was physically present in the store, but her thoughts remained behind with her daughter. A lady who was standing in the checkout line noticed the sadness on my friend's face. And that's when the well-meaning, foolish words were uttered: "Smile! C'mon, life can't be that bad."

The lady is lucky Johanna didn't target her forehead with canned goods. Instead, Johanna graciously chose to ignore the trite comment.

Foolish words spray out of our mouths when we lack gentleness. A gentle spirit would have led the lady at the store to say a silent prayer, pat my friend on her shoulder, or even pay for my friend's groceries.

Gentleness puts us in others' shoes. It makes no assumptions. It softens our hearts that we might soften others'. And God gives us the strength to step out of our bubbles and into people's hurts.

God exhibited both strength and gentleness to my friends. Not only did he sustain them through the trial, he surprised the medical professionals by miraculously healing their daughter.

// SPIRITUAL LAZINESS

Physical training is of some value, but godliness has value for all things, holding promise for both the present life and the life to come.

1 TIMOTHY 4:8

For a number of years, I lifted weights very early in the morning. My workout partner and I gave nicknames to many of the entertaining characters in the gym. Some of the guys were just funny. The Grunters made sure everyone knew how hard they were straining. If a man were to give birth to a cow, he would probably sound like those guys. But we wondered why some of the other guys even came.

Newspaper Man showed up a few minutes after us every day. He would change into workout clothes in the locker room and then emerge with a rubber-banded newspaper. He'd then sit on the bench-press bench and find the sports page. After about fifteen minutes, he'd switch locations, do one rep of lifting, and then dive back into the *Tulsa World*. He averaged about three minutes of exercise per hour. We imagined his conversations with his wife: "It's so crazy; I've been going to the gym every day for a year, and I just can't lose the weight."

Slippers Dude was the best. He was there before we got there and there when we left. We never saw him do a single exercise. To his credit, he never even pretended. He shuffled around in his house shoes, telling the same old jokes to the Grunters, Newspaper Man, and every other soul in the gym. Everyone loved him, although I'm not sure they wanted to copy his regimen.

Paul instructed Timothy that physical training is of some value.[4] Indeed, healthy training can increase the health of our emotions and empower us to help others. Educational training is also of some value. Paul's education gave him a voice with the philosophers, teachers, and cultural elites of his day. Education enables people to increase their understanding of humankind, solve problems of their day, and add beauty to the world. There are many areas in which growth is of some value. We pursue these areas as much as we can, but we remember the word *some*. These things are of *some* value. So when we get lazy with them, there are certainly *some* consequences. We see them all the time.

Paul wrote on to Timothy, "But godliness has value for all things, holding promise for both the present life and the life to come." While many pursuits can add value, healing, and peace to our fractured world, godliness must be our greatest pursuit. When we become lazy in our desire for godliness, the consequences are eternal.

The other day I talked with a man who confessed, "I've gotten lazy with God." Most of the people I know who fell away from God never made a conscious decision to do so. Instead, they just slowly faded away. They grew lazy in their commitments. They quit reading their Bibles, praying, worshiping with their church families, and prioritizing their small-group relationships. Little by little, they drifted away. When some Highland Park members knocked on the man's door one Saturday, they just asked him if they could pray for him. In that moment, God got his attention. He told me, "I'm so excited—I can feel God closing the distance between the two of us. I feel my insecurities washing away. I know I need to recommit to weekly encouragement and daily disciplines. I know I need to start serving people again. I know I need to start caring for people again. And I'm ready to begin."

Spiritual laziness erodes our strength and gentleness. It causes apathy, frustration, and selfishness. We don't conquer spiritual laziness on our own. In fact, attempts to rely on our own strength separate us from godliness. But Christ will work mightily through our weaknesses, and he'll transform our limited strength into his unlimited potential. I believe the man I met will unleash God's strength and gentleness in his workplace and home.

Let me add one more word of caution here: The stronger we become in the things that add *some* value, the more tempted we might be to use them against others. The financially strong so often oppress the poor. The educationally strong snub the uneducated. The physically strong intimidate the weak. So be careful to not weaponize the things of *some value*. Instead, pursue godliness above all things, and God himself will clothe you with strength and gentleness.

A BETTER DAY

I long for better days. I long for days when we see people like Doug everywhere, full of strong gentleness and gentle strength. I long for days when people walk into grocery stores, ready to say a gentle word to any hurting soul. I long for days when our culture values gentleness above bravado and loving strength above brute force. I long for days when I sense God's slightest nudge, and, like a great horse, I immediately walk in his direction. I long for the days when we have the strength to climb out of our bunkers, and we have the gentleness to live in peace with each other. I long for the days of dancing in no man's land.

I think you long for these days too. So let's turn to the one who guides us there: our Good Shepherd, the Gentle King.

REFLECTION QUESTIONS

1. When have you seen gentleness and strength exemplified?

2. Do you think you're more like the horse needing a whip or more like the horse sensing God's gentle nudges? Can you think of examples?

3. Which of the three "enemies of gentle strength" poses the biggest threat to you? Selfishness, insensitivity, or spiritual laziness?

4. How is Jesus the Good Shepherd? What does that look like practically in your life?

5. Thank God for being our Gentle King and tell him your heart is open to being filled with his gentleness and strength.

CHAPTER 10

CONVICTION AND DISCERNMENT

This is my prayer: that your love may abound more and more in knowledge and depth of insight, so that you may be able to discern what is best and may be pure and blameless for the day of Christ, filled with the fruit of righteousness that comes through Jesus Christ—to the glory and praise of God.

PHILIPPIANS 1:9-11

BETH AND I TOOK OUR oldest kids to watch *The Heart of Man*, a movie you should move to the top of your must-watch-soon list. In a breathtakingly beautiful way, the movie tells of God's unending love for us, even in our brokenness. In the movie, my friend Tony Anderson tells how God revealed a beautiful lesson to him. After a day of regret, he felt the shackles of shame around him. He pictured himself as a prisoner, looking for a place to sit in the prison cafeteria. Jesus comes, dressed as a fellow prisoner, and eats lunch with him. Tony appreciates his kindness, and Jesus says, "You can eat lunch with me anytime. The door is right over there, and it's open. You can walk out of here anytime."

Tony shared how God is with us, even in our sin. This statement led to a great conversation in our car on the way home:

"Isn't God holy, 'set apart'?" one of my children asked. Yes. Jesus died for our sin, so we must never underestimate the treachery of sin and the perfection of God.

"But Tony said God is with us when we sin," another noted. "Is that true?" Yes. It is. If God weren't with us in our sin, we wouldn't read much about him from Genesis 3 to Revelation 20. God keeps entering the picture of sinful humankind. He didn't exit the story when David committed adultery with Bathsheba. He was there to hear David's heart-wrenching confession (Psalm 51). Jesus didn't exit the story when his closest friends sinned against him. He went to people like the Samaritan woman and the denying Peter, even in their shame.

How do we handle tensions like this? Well, we leave the tension alone. No man's land is a place where we hold our deepest convictions, even when they fit clumsily in our hands. We can say with conviction, "God is holy," while also declaring, "He's with us in our sin." The first statement doesn't mean God runs from us at the first sign of trouble. The second doesn't mean he's unconcerned with sin. Both statements of conviction are true, so it will take discernment to know how to live in the tension.

Conviction is a belief you'll hang on to until your dying breath. Discernment is the ability to judge well, including the wisdom to decide if something ought to be a conviction. Jesus demonstrated both in a story that perfectly captures the heart of this book.

TAXES AND TRAPS

The Pharisees, Herodians, and Sadducees battled for power and position among the Jewish people. These religious authorities constantly swayed people into their bunkers, slaying anyone found on the other side. But in Mark 12, the opposing parties joined forces with one goal: trap Jesus. Matthew, Mark, and Luke all record the scheme:

> Later they sent some of the Pharisees and Herodians to Jesus to catch him in his words. They came to him and said, "Teacher, we know that you are a man of integrity. You aren't swayed by others, because you pay no attention to who they are; but you teach the way of God in accordance with the truth. Is it right to pay the imperial tax to Caesar or not? Should we pay or shouldn't we?"[1]

Taxes were a sensitive topic among the Jewish people under Roman rule. As the Roman Empire expanded, Caesar Augustus appointed kings, governors, and officials to collect the taxes and tribute for him. Those appointed officials tarnished the system. They learned that if they collected more tax money than needed, they could pocket the difference. For officials and tax collectors, cheating became the norm. For the common man, poverty became the norm. Everyone could see the problem, cheated and cheater alike.

Around the time of Christ's birth, Publius Varus governed Syria on behalf of Rome. It was said about him, "As a poor man he went to a rich province, and as a rich man left a poor province."[2] Herod oversaw the Palestinian area. He brutalized the people, collecting mass sums from them to build elaborate palaces for himself. The people were taxed unto poverty, hunger, sickness, and even death.

With hopes of undoing Herod's corruption, the Jews sent a delegation to complain to Caesar. He had no way of validating their complaints without knowing the population data. So . . .

In those days Caesar Augustus issued a decree that a census
should be taken of the entire Roman world.
LUKE 2:1

They collected data, but three decades later, corruption remained. The Roman officials continued to mistreat those they governed, especially the Jews.

Making matters immeasurably worse, the caesars claimed to be not only political leaders but also gods. Even their currency proclaimed this.

In a world with no newspapers or social media, Caesar Augustus and Mark Antony began the practice of issuing coins containing a picture and a few words of propaganda. At the time of our story, Pilate oversaw taxation of the Jews. He agitated them, issuing coins that claimed Roman divinity.[3]

The probable coin collected for tax and presented to Jesus was a silver denarius. The coin boasted Tiberius Caesar's claim of godhood by displaying his portrait with a laurel wreath. The inscription read "Emperor Tiberius Son of the Divine Augustus." The inscription on the back of the coin boasted, "Most High Priest."

These coins incensed the Jews, but religious leaders had different stances about how they should respond. The debate ignited: "Should we pay this tax or not?"

A segment of Jewish leaders believed the people ought to pay their taxes. Doing so, they said, honored God with good citizenry. Most Jews followed this advice. Joseph and Mary's laborious trek to Bethlehem, while Mary was about to give birth to Jesus, indicates that they were in this camp.

Another segment of Jewish leaders rebelled. A scribe named Judas of Galilee called on his countrymen to revolt against the tax and thus against the empire.[4] He argued if you paid taxes to Caesar, you were a coward, submitting to mere mortals as opposed to God. Judas established a headquarters and was joined by a number of supporters, including many Pharisees. Their protest garnered enough attention that the Romans attacked, killing Judas and many of his followers.

When the religious leaders posed the question to Jesus—"Should we pay taxes or not?"—it came loaded with emotion and danger. If Jesus said yes, it would sound like an endorsement of Caesar's claim to divinity. Who would want a Messiah who cowered before Caesar? But if Jesus said no, he'd be killed for rebellion against Rome. Jesus' adversaries thought they'd finally rigged an unescapable trap—forcing Jesus to choose a bunker. But they didn't plan on Jesus' discernment amidst his convictions.

INTERPRETING

Beth, my wife, holds a degree in sign language interpretation. Her professors impressed upon the students that interpreters don't have the right to soften or strengthen language. Beth even had to learn a slew of vulgar words one day, which she describes as the most awkward hour of her education. That day's lesson held value, because good interpreters serve as conduits, not filters, of communication. And like it or not, every time you read your Bible, you are interpreting.

Years ago, some funny guys from a church voiced over a series of clips from the original *JESUS* film.[5] They gave Jesus a wimpy voice and snooty personality, making him say things like "John, you drank too much wine the other night, not way too much, just enough to make me angry." When I first viewed the clips, I wasn't sure if I should be offended or laugh out loud. Laughter won out.

The videos drive home a point: When anyone, including a movie director, tells you about Jesus, they are actually telling you their interpretation of Jesus. The interpretation of Scripture may or may not communicate what the author intended. The best interpretations achieve a level of noninterference, just as a good sign-language interpreter would not interfere with the communicator's words and intent.

Movies and pictures often portray Jesus as a bit of a sissy, which is a terrible interpretation. Equally terrible is a picture of Jesus dressed like Rambo. But it's not hard to imagine two opposing religious bunkers, both with a narrow and wrong interpretation of Jesus. Admitting we interpret Scripture when we read it gets us started on a good path to no man's land.

The two groups of religious leaders in Mark 12 both read the Scriptures, but they'd interpreted themselves into bunkers. When they plotted together to trick Jesus, they assumed there was no possible way to interpret the Scriptures without an extreme view. Nuance was nowhere in sight.

Jesus consistently had the fortitude and wits to stand strong and still in no man's land. To escape the bunkers of the tricksters, he'd have to correctly interpret Scriptures. But that's not all he'd need.

CONVICTION

If you were to name your top five convictions, what would be on your list?

- Trust God?
- Commit to family?

- Work hard?
- Relax?
- Find good pizza?

Our convictions are a line in the sand for us. We don't compromise them. They are core values we never violate, right?

Peter and John's convictions were put to the test shortly after the church began. They were preaching in Jerusalem, and many people were responding to the new Good News about Jesus. The religious rulers brought Peter and John in, questioned them, and warned them against preaching anymore. Peter's reply is one for the ages: "Which is right in God's eyes: to listen to you, or to him? You be the judges! As for us, we cannot help speaking about what we have seen and heard" (Acts 4:19-20). Peter and John held a deep conviction: Obedience to God trumps obedience to humans. There are times to be silent, to say, "Yes, sir," and move on. But discernment tells us there are also times to say, "Your demands of me collide with my deepest convictions, God's commands, so I choose God." Peter and John didn't unnecessarily offend or insult the rulers, but they made their convictions gently, firmly known. They would keep preaching about Jesus, for choosing silence would be crossing their line in the sand. So convictions are easy to honor, right?

Well, not always. Sometimes our convictions collide. I've committed to give my very best to our church. I've also committed to never trade my family for work or career success. My job gives me the option to work more, every single day of every single week. I could always visit one more person, study for one more sermon, or encourage one more leader. It's why so many preachers have personally crashed or just walked away. (With the advancement of technology, more and more jobs offer the same potential to overwork.) Beth has heard me ask lots of questions such as "Mike is in the hospital—should I leave the family gathering early or stay here?" or "Mitchel and Yarah asked me to do their wedding in June, and my schedule that month is already crazy, so what do you think?" When convictions collide, we pray for discernment.

Some convictions I can choose to neatly keep every day, such as loving God and loving others. Other convictions, such as giving my best at home and work, won't look tidy on a daily basis, even if I do my best. However, I'd rather evaluate these convictions with a wider lens, maybe at the end of the month or year.

Our family watched a tightrope act in Branson, Missouri, one time. Branson is a family place, and I assumed the performers would be attached to safety harnesses, or that there would at least be a net below. Nope. Nothing. I spent an hour praying my kids wouldn't spend the rest of their lives recovering from witnessing a horrific death. We clapped every time they didn't die, which seems to be a ridiculous form of entertainment to me.

If I had to walk on a tightrope, I'd want to hold on to something. If there were a rope coming from the right and another coming from the left, I could hold both and balance. I'd want both of them to offer a little bit of tension. This is how I picture managing life's convictions. If I feel zero pull to spend time at home, it's probably a sign that I'm letting myself be pulled too hard at work. A little bit of tension from both directions offers healthy balance. So when you think about the tension with your convictions, give yourself some grace. Honor your convictions, but also welcome the balance a little bit of tension can offer.

If Jesus was going to survive the question of "Should we pay taxes or not?" he'd need to manage deep convictions. But that's not all.

DISCERNMENT

Lance Armstrong used to be my hero. Over the span of one decade, he crushed the world's greatest bicyclists, the world's most excruciating bike race, and one of the world's most feared diseases. He also crushed anyone who threatened to expose his secret.

Armstrong's popularity skyrocketed after he overcame cancer. When he started stockpiling yellow jerseys (victories) at the Tour de France, he became one of the most popular figures in the world. I'll never forget watching a grueling mountain stage in which a bystander's bag snagged his handlebars. Armstrong toppled to the ground, losing valuable seconds. Once back on his bike, adrenaline surged through his body. He danced on his pedals until he caught the race leaders, but he didn't slow down. Soon, the rest of the field could only see the back of his jersey. Armstrong seemed invincible.

As his victories grew, whispers of performance-enhancing drugs surfaced. Soon, accusations and investigations dogged his every step. Armstrong, as he always did, fought back and won. He attacked his accusers with the same ferocity with which he attacked the steep inclines of the Alps. Those not defending Armstrong's integrity risked their reputations, jobs, and financial security. Armstrong seemed invincible.

But in 2013, Armstrong crashed. This time there'd be no recovery. Evidence forced him to reveal years of doping. He'd cheated. He'd used, exploited, and ruined people. Armstrong was a fake. People like me, his fans, felt shocked. Then we felt anger. We'd been duped.

Lance Armstrong's tumble reminded me of the value of discernment. In this case, I lacked it. We need to beg God to give us discernment, so we can protect the innocent and see deceivers for who they are.

Discernment gives us a clearer view of others' motives. It guides us to know if we should pray for the deceiver privately or expose the danger publicly. It lets parents know if their teen is complimenting them or just buttering them up. It helps the leader know if their underachieving employee needs a compassionate ear or a firm rebuke. It informs us of the answer to U2's melodious question: "Is there a time for keeping your mouth shut; is this the time for [speaking up about] human rights?"[6] Jesus possessed discernment in full. People betrayed, denied, and lied to him, but nobody successfully duped the only innocent man to ever live.

A THIRD OPTION

When the religious leaders were waiting for Jesus to respond to their trick question, they readied themselves to pounce. Pulling a page out of Daniel's book, Jesus asked a question: "Whose picture do you see?"

"Caesar's," they replied.

"So give back to Caesar what is Caesar's, and to God what is God's."[7]

Jesus affirmed Caesar's finite political authority, but God's infinite authority. "Caesar designed a coin. Big deal. Give it back. Pay your taxes. But God made you, so give your whole self to him." Jesus showed discernment in his response without sacrificing conviction. He offered an alternative path, refusing to lunge for the cheese on the trap.

How quickly do you take the bait? Are you quick to believe one side of the story? Do you side with defamation and libel on the Internet? Do you lean in when you hear gossip? How quickly do you bite and get bunkered?

If you look hard enough, you can often find an alternate path into no man's land. Most of the easy-to-see paths will eventually give way to slippery slopes. They'll send you sliding down into a bunker. Seek the alternative. Don't settle for the easy route, the obvious way.

For example, when someone rips into a coworker, you could reframe his or her agenda: "I'd encourage you to visit with him. You might be able to really help him and our company." In two short sentences, you've revealed your convictions to care for both the company and your coworkers. You've also revealed your discernment to not bite when someone offers slander or gossip.

Or when two friends ask your input into their dispute over the latest news story, you could say, "We know the media portrays the opinions of those on the extreme edges, but I wonder what sincere questions those without their minds already made up are asking." In a simple observation, you've communicated that everyone's convictions should be heard so that discernment can be exercised about the best path forward.

Yes. I know. The two examples may cause social awkwardness. Instead of running for cover, be confident, calm, and committed.

Be confident. If the "alternate path" is really a better path, confidence will fill you.

Be calm. Expect people to react when they see you standing in no man's land. That's okay. It may be their first glimpse of anyone living in the middle.

Be committed. Living in no man's land is the right thing to do, even if others give you funny looks. Encouraging others to exit their bunkers will take time. The most powerful moments may come after your encounter, as they ponder your strange ways.

SOMEONE TO TRUST

Our dear friend Susie is a dance instructor. If I spun like her, I'd lose both my balance and my lunch. But she makes it look graceful and easy. She says the secret is to pick out one prominent, stationary object in the room and to focus on it every time around. By seeing the object, she stays oriented and balanced. I pray you know where to look to get your bearings. The Bible describes God as our Rock (Psalm 18:31). The waves may crash or we may spin, but he's steady, secure, true. If your greatest conviction is that God is your Rock, you'll find the discernment to move forward. You'll hold truth and peace in the same hand.

Jesus' discernment never undermined his convictions. Mark 12 wasn't the last time he'd be asked about taxes. Later in his ministry, tax collectors came to Peter, asking if Jesus paid his taxes.[8] Jesus, as he'd done before, told Peter they did. He then instructed Peter to go to the lake, catch a fish, and look in its mouth. Peter obeyed and found a coin in the fish's mouth. Now that's a great fishing story—and it's true.

Obedience leads us to find God's provision in the most surprising places. If you choose to live in no man's land, embracing conviction and discernment in a hostile world, sometimes you'll need a miracle. Take hope: You'll find God in this land between.

REFLECTION QUESTIONS

1. What are your top five convictions?

2. When have your convictions collided?

3. Name some modern-day examples of the "Should you pay taxes or not?" question that bait people into bunkers.

4. Are you a discerning person?

5. Ask God to guide your convictions and discernment so you can follow him even when tricksters surround you.

CHAPTER 11

SHREWDNESS AND INNOCENCE

I am sending you out like sheep among wolves. Therefore be as shrewd as snakes and as innocent as doves.

MATTHEW 10:16

WHEN JESUS SENT OUT THE disciples on a mission trip, he warned of danger. He instructed them to be as shrewd as snakes and as innocent as doves.

I'm okay with the part about doves.

Years ago in Manila, Philippines, I spent eight days teaching youth ministry and Bible classes with a great organization, Christ In Youth. We partnered with a local Bible college, and I loved getting to know many of their students. During my first meal in their cafeteria, one story headlined the conversations. The students raised pigs to offset tuition costs, so they were upset to learn that a king cobra had killed one of their pigs. I, too, was upset, but for a different reason. Suddenly, death-by-cobra was now a possibility in my life. I'd really been trying to avoid that reality.

We played basketball on their outdoor courts during class breaks. I reveled in my height—this was the first time in my life I was the tallest person on the court. When one of our shots ricocheted off the rim and into a field of tall weeds, I bounded after it.

Midstride, the sudden awareness of my predicament jolted my body. I was in a field of waist-high weeds. Near the pig barn.

With only one foot on the ground, I froze.

I saw no sign of the snake, but all I could think about was how big, scary, and deadly it must be. I thought about how snakes like tall grass. I thought about my family and friends. I thought about the pain of getting struck. I thought about how slow traffic moved on the crowded Manila streets and how far away medical help must be. I wondered if venom and death feel icy when they course through a body.

Hissssssssss!

One of the students had correctly guessed why I froze. He must have seen the terror on my face and had snuck up behind me to hiss. The memory still makes me sweat.

The students fell down in laughter. I laughed too, but only after my feet returned to the ground and scampered back to the pavement.

Even though many of us detest snakes, Jesus told the disciples to emulate serpentine shrewdness. With persecution looming, false teachers manipulating, and throngs of people seeking truth, the disciples needed more than innocent motives. They had to be prepared to make shrewd, strategic, calculated decisions.

They would need Paul's shrewdness, like when he mentioned to his Roman captors, "Hey, did you know you just mistreated me, a Roman citizen? I hope your commanders do not find out, because you know what will happen to you."[1] They'd need to be shrewd like Stephen when he used the whole of Jewish history to rebuke Jewish leaders.[2] They would need to be shrewd like Jesus when he buried cunning trouble-makers in their own trick questions.[3]

Shrewdness is the ability to make wise, strategic, effective plans— and to do so quickly when needed. When we think of innocence, we picture a child—pure, without guile, authentic. Shrewdness on its own can be manipulation. Innocence on its own can be naiveté. But put them together, and you've added an invaluable tool to your belt. Purity of heart along with strategic acumen dwells in the leaders of no man's land.

When hostility surrounds you, you'll need more than a white flag to broker peace. You'll need wisdom and wits, along with your white flag. Effective peacemakers craft a plan.

DIFFERENT STROKES

You can't find a one-size-fits-all response to hostile situations. You'll have to survey the land to determine the most God-honoring path toward love. Jesus' innocent shrewdness led him to choose different responses.

// 1. SOMETIMES JESUS REBUKED.

When Jesus witnessed the unfair, cheating, exclusive practices of those who had turned the Temple into a den of thieves, a quiet discussion would not suffice. He flipped tables, cracked a whip, and chased people away. We know he successfully got their attention because Mark 11:18 says, "The whole crowd was amazed at his teaching" and describes others plotting his death.

On another occasion, Jesus verbally unloaded. Matthew 23 contains Jesus' longest and sharpest rebukes. Read it and you'll be surprised by his words to the hypocritical religious leaders.

At the age of eleven, I went on a weekend trip with my dad and a bunch of other guys from church. On the way back home, late Saturday night, one of Dad's friends rode with us. My head rested on a pillow, and they both assumed I was asleep. I lack the gift of being able to sleep in moving cars, but I'm quite skilled at eavesdropping.

Dad's friend began complaining about our preacher, Randy. His main gripe was that Randy preached too much about evangelism.[4] I'll never forget Dad's calm, firm rebuke: "First, I disagree with you. Second, you need to go speak with Randy. Jesus taught us in Matthew 18 to go directly to the person with whom we have a complaint."

Awkwardness swallowed the car.

I kept my eyes closed, but I wanted to cheer.

Dad's friend gave it one more attempt, trying with all his might to convince Dad to join his side of the argument. No one likes to complain alone.

Once again, Dad refused.

I remember lots of silence after that. Choosing the road less traveled leads to awkward, uncomfortable moments. But Dad's shepherding of the church continued, and Randy kept preaching *too much* about evangelism.

Sometimes a rebuke is needed, but don't rush here too quickly. Jesus rebuked the religious leaders who mistreated others, but he never rebuked the vulnerable, confused, and hurting people who did not know God. Shrewdness means knowing when to step forward with hard words and when to hold back. Being innocent means our intentions are never to harm a person for our own glory but to protect the flock and confront the perpetrators with their need for repentance.

// 2. SOMETIMES JESUS IGNORED, REDIRECTED, OR CONFUSED.

When religious leaders asked Jesus from where he received his authority, they hoped to hang him with his answer. (At this point, I'm starting to picture them as Wile E. Coyote, that cartoon character whose schemes always backfired.) What do you suppose Jesus did? By this point, you should know: Instead of answering the question, Jesus replied, "I will ask you one question. Answer me, and I will tell you by what authority I am doing these things" (Mark 11:29).

He proceeded to ask them a question that turned the tables. They realized they were trapped and exposed, so they chose silence. Jesus responded, "Neither will I tell you by what authority I am doing these things" (verse 33).

When charlatans ask you a question, you might be wise to choose silence. It may be the firmest reply you can give.

Other times, Jesus redirected their question or just gave an answer that left everyone confused. He knew a direct answer would do no good in the ears of a fool. As Proverbs 23:9 tells us, "Do not speak to fools, for they will scorn your prudent words."

You'll need shrewdness to know when an answer will do more harm than good, and you'll need innocence to not resent the people asking.

// 3. SOMETIMES JESUS ANSWERED CLEARLY.

In Mark 12:18-27, the Sadducees, who were skeptics of any future resurrection, asked Jesus about his beliefs on the subject. That tells us about everything we need to know about their motives. They made up a long-winded hypothetical situation: If a woman's husband died, and then she remarried but that man also died, and she remarried but that third man *also* died, etc., who would be her husband in the life to come? Jesus responded without a parable or veiled story. He chose to plainly answer them, while also correcting their false teaching about the resurrection. He sums up his response: "You are badly mistaken." Plain. Simple. To the point.

Without innocence, we'll mistreat people with our answers. The person with guile assumes he or she is better than the rest. Without shrewdness, our answers will wound people or exacerbate the problem. Jesus responded to people with both innocence and shrewdness, which let him pursue truth and peace in hostile crowds. How they responded was up to them, but he always chose the noble, best path, which most people never even saw as an option until he showed them the way.

PARTY CRASHER

Jesus eagerly accepted invites to parties, and in Luke 7, he dined with a Pharisee. Simon's party would have garnered much attention, which made it a perfect place to teach a lesson the viewers would never forget. Jesus even demonstrated shrewdness with his dinner plans. In the middle of the meal, an uninvited woman crashed the party. And not just any woman. Luke doesn't identify her sin, but it seems likely she was a prostitute. Whatever her sin, we know from the text that it was infamously bad. Her guilty reputation preceded her.

It may seem odd that she barged into the party, but it was common for a host to allow others access to a meal in honor of a popular figure. The woman may have been observing their dinner through a window. No one seemed shocked at her presence, but her antics left them aghast.

> She came there with an alabaster jar of perfume. As she stood behind [Jesus] at his feet weeping, she began to wet his feet with her tears. Then she wiped them with her hair, kissed them and poured perfume on them.
>
> LUKE 7:37-38

The upscale meal turned scandal.

The woman's actions reflected sacrifice, tender care, and unbridled emotion. The perfume she poured on his feet was precious and expensive. This type of anointing was traditionally reserved for the purifying of priests or the Tabernacle.[5] The perfume may have cost a year's salary per pound.[6] Everything about her actions—the undoing of her hair, the kissing of his feet, and the pouring of the perfume—offended the dinner party. *Oh, the nerve of that woman. She surely realizes how others are viewing her, right?*

Simon reacted first. He blamed Jesus for this outrage. He revealed his lack of faith in Jesus: "If this man were a prophet, he would know who is touching him and what kind of woman she is—that she is a sinner." He transferred the shame of the unclean woman onto his supposedly honored guest.

In a satisfying twist of irony, Jesus read his mind. Simon made a theological assumption: Holy, innocent people reject sinners. And there sat Jesus, on earth, surrounded by sinners, telling another story:

> Two people owed money to a certain moneylender. One owed him five hundred denarii, and the other fifty. Neither of them had the money to pay him back, so he forgave the debts of both. Now which of them will love him more?
>
> LUKE 7:41-42

Passion envelops the story. Imagine the appreciation and love flowing from the one who had been forgiven a great debt. The debtor lacked any bargaining power. Mercy offered his only hope, and mercy is what he got. The mercy he received produced great love.

One time my son gave sixty dollars to Blackbox International (the ministry we support that helps trafficked boys) as a Father's Day gift to me. My first impulse was to tell him it was too much, and that he shouldn't give away his entire piggy bank of chore money. Only someone with innocent, unadulterated generosity does such a thing. I'm glad I bit my tongue and let him worship Jesus.

The woman's actions proved she understood Jesus. Meanwhile, Simon simmered with disdain, so Jesus cranked up the thermostat.

> Then he turned toward the woman and said to Simon, "Do you see this woman? I came into your house. You did not give me any water for my feet, but she wet my feet with her tears and wiped them with her hair. You did not give me a kiss, but this woman, from the time I entered, has not stopped kissing my feet. You did not put oil on my head, but she has poured perfume on my feet."
>
> LUKE 7:44-46

The woman showered him with love, while Simon neglected the customary acts of hospitality. Showering one person with gentleness may require rebuking someone else. Shrewdness and innocence echoed through the room at the same time. The same words that embraced the woman slammed Simon with a convicting force. Judgment often comes with two edges—the crashing waves can crush some while saving others. The double-edged sword of Jesus simultaneously rescued and rebuked.

DOUBLE-EDGED SWORD

A few weeks ago the *Wall Street Journal*'s front page picture brought me to a screeching halt in a busy Starbucks. The picture showed a refugee holding his baby, who'd died when their boat sank just a few meters from shore. I can still see the horror in his eyes. Pure devastation. Jesus saw a similar look of desperation when he saw Jairus. His twelve-year-old daughter was dying, his world was shattering, and he was begging Jesus to heal his girl. Jesus said yes.[7]

While still on their way, word came that Jairus' daughter was already dead. It was too late. However, Jesus, with a calm that made no sense, said, "Just believe." They continued on to Jairus's house.

When they arrived, the family's grieving was in full force, but Jesus told them not to worry, saying the girl was just sleeping. The crowd laughed at Jesus' suggestion, so Jesus ordered them to leave the house. Now, with just the mom, dad, dead girl, and a few disciples, he took the girl by the hand and brought her back to life. Then he told them to not tell anyone. He loved healing people, but his primary purpose was spiritual. Jesus was so perfectly innocent, he risked jeopardizing his ministry to show compassion to a grieving father, and he was so full of shrewdness that he could rebuke a crowd and caution a family.

My parents recall snickering with other back-row teenagers at the young man who used to go forward, every single Sunday, during the church's invitation time. The troubled man struggled to convey his thoughts and often repeated the same things. The teenagers relished the moment, but the words of their preacher, Boyce Mouton, silenced their giggles. Boyce would wax eloquent about how much God appreciated soft hearts, acts of confession, and compassion for the hurting. He'd quote Scriptures, and then he'd pray with his arm around the man. By the time he was done, the teens felt about six inches tall. Judgment often comes with two edges—the words that lift one up from the depths can cut another down to size.

Do Jesus' words convict you? Would anger swell within you if Jesus gave attention to someone you abhor?

Jesus' diverse approaches to volatile circumstances demonstrate his shrewdness and wisdom. Yet his heart for peace, love, and healing never wavers.

GET TO WORK

Take a minute to jot down a list of cunning, shrewd people in your life. Then jot down a list of people in your life with hearts of gold. Seriously, get a pen and piece of paper and do it.

Take your time.

Did anyone appear on both lists? Would your friends include your name on either list?

We see foolish people with great hearts, but foolish people can't broker peace. They don't know how. Years ago I was volunteering with an organization helping at-risk children. When two kids started fighting, I intervened, but the fight only escalated. Now three people were getting punched. I should have stayed seated. I only made matters worse. A terrible strategy accompanied my impeccable intentions. I lacked the foresight and insight to help the situation.

We also see crafty people with dubious motives. Untrustworthy people won't lead us to peace, either—in fact, they'll stir the flames. Two spoiled brats on the playground can't share the only swing, let alone decide which kid should get the next turn. It's not within them any more than it is for selfish spouses to start serving each other. Without a change on the inside, peace will always break apart on the outside.

Jesus calls for his disciples to demonstrate two exceptional qualities rarely found together. Peacemakers study his every move. Sometimes plain, straightforward language works best. Sometimes a rebuke is in order. Sometimes a story suffices. Sometimes silence speaks the loudest. Your path forward will often lack clarity, so beg God for shrewdness. You'll be tempted to abuse your power, exaggerate a story, or manipulate a friendship, so beg God for innocence. Refuse to believe you must choose one or the other. Value both; dance with both. Lead us to peace and truth.

REFLECTION QUESTIONS

1. Is there a part of you that reacts against the command to be either shrewd or innocent? Which one? Why?

2. How do you typically respond to questions that might bait you into a bunker?

3. Has there been a recent time you wished you would've responded to a question as Jesus demonstrated? How so?

4. Did you make the list of those with shrewdness and those with innocence? What did you discover?

5. How can you grow in shrewdness and innocence? Pray for your mind and heart to be like Jesus'. Write down one commitment you'll make to grow in both areas this week.

CHAPTER 12

HUMILITY AND COURAGE

——

Brothers and sisters, think of what you were when you were called. Not many of you were wise by human standards; not many were influential; not many were of noble birth. But God chose the foolish things of the world to shame the wise; God chose the weak things of the world to shame the strong. God chose the lowly things of this world and the despised things—and the things that are not—to nullify the things that are, so that no one may boast before him. It is because of him that you are in Christ Jesus, who has become for us wisdom from God—that is, our righteousness, holiness and redemption. Therefore, as it is written: "Let the one who boasts boast in the Lord."

I CORINTHIANS 1:26-31

WHEN I FIRST CAME TO TULSA, the wise counsel and gentle spirit of Chuck Thomas drew me to him. His sweet wife, Anita, passed away after a long, discouraging illness. If his wife's illness was the final exam of his vows, he aced it. He loved her in sickness, until death parted them.

When Chuck passed away, I stood next to his body in the hospital for a few minutes before his family arrived. I thought about how Chuck prayed for my family every day, and I wondered how many times God's answers to those prayers kept me afloat during difficult days. Chuck also hungered for God's Word. He daily dived into it, pen at the ready.

One time while Chuck was recovering from a surgery, he told me a story I'd never heard. While in Bible college, Chuck was invited to preach at the First Christian Church near Gotebo, Oklahoma, for several

Sundays while they searched for a new preacher. Chuck accepted the interim position and drove to the small town the following Sunday.

The church (both the building and the people) seemed split down the middle. Each side had its own Communion table, and each side had elders who separately prayed and served their half of the congregation. This strange division bewildered Chuck and Anita.

A friendly family invited them over for Sunday lunch. After eating, Chuck asked about the obvious division. To his surprise, the family knew there was a division, but they didn't know why. So they got on the phone and tracked down the answer from their grandmother.

Many years earlier, the congregation voted to install new carpet. Half of the congregation wanted blue carpet, but the other half wanted rose carpet. The dispute led to a split church. They put blue carpet in half of the church building and rose carpet in the other half. Families stayed on *their* carpet and only shared Communion with their like-minded friends. Even after the carpet was updated, folks kept to their sides.

One church. Two bunkers.

Chuck's a mild-mannered guy, but God whispered for him to pick up his prophet's staff. With trembling hands, he obeyed.

Chuck had already planned to preach on the Lord's Prayer from Matthew 6 the following week. He narrowed his text to one line of Jesus' prayer: "Father, forgive us our debts, as we forgive our debtors." He pleaded with them to forgive anyone needing forgiveness.

The next week he preached about forgiveness again.

And the next week, again.

After the third consecutive forgiveness sermon, the elders decided it was time for a chat. They asked him why he was spending so much time on that one specific phrase from the Lord's Prayer.

Chuck conveyed his anguish about their unforgiving attitude. He said, "If we won't forgive those who offend us, God won't forgive us. I feel compelled to keep preaching this until y'all forgive each other."

The next Sunday, things were going as usual. The people took their places, and Chuck slid Forgiveness Sermon Number Four into his Bible. *Here we go again*, he thought.

But when it came time for Communion, hearts yielded to the Spirit. One of the elders, with tears in his eyes, wailed, "Wait! I can't do this anymore." He walked to the other side, extended his hand, and asked one of the other elders for forgiveness.

The other elder did not offer his hand. He embraced him with both arms.

People in the congregation started doing the same thing. Forgiveness was requested and granted. Tears flowed. Joy erupted.

By the time people returned to their seats, it was almost lunchtime. Chuck pulled his sermon notes out of his Bible and tossed them on the pew. He walked to the pulpit, read the Lord's Prayer, and dismissed them with prayer. And for the first time in years, they went home in peace.

Chuck's eyes paraded his delight as he finished the story. "Can you believe I would be such a brash kid? Can you believe I'd do that kind of thing? But it was one of the greatest moments of my life."

Chuck wasn't brash. He was courageous enough to do what was right, and he was humble enough to give God all the credit—a rare combination. Chuck stood in no man's land. He risked making enemies from both bunkers. He spoke truth and it led to peace.

Paul told the church in Corinth to only boast in the Lord. He wanted the church leaders to redirect any praise that came their way. It was a call to humility. These leaders were boldly preaching Christ, even when it was wildly unpopular. They were courageous, and they needed to combine that trait with humility.

The humble person considers others better than himself or herself (Philippians 2:3-4). Chuck preached about forgiveness because he cared for the people more than he cared for himself and he placed God's Word above his own security and comfort. Humility makes it easier to have courage. Humility frees you from fretting about what others think about you and releases you from fear.

The courageous person does what is right in spite of fear. Erwin McManus wrote, "Courage is not the absence of fear; it is the absence of self."[1] You were created to be courageous. "For the Spirit God gave us does not make us timid, but gives us power, love and self-discipline" (2 Timothy 1:7).

LESS IS MORE

Humility and courage are so important because not only are they prerequisites for no man's land, but if we lack them, we'll damage people. People with humility and courage lay some things on the altar to be killed. They know that sometimes, less is more.

// SPEECH-LESS

I do not want to wound more people. I want to help more people. I'm learning that a lot of the words that form in my head need to die before they make it to my mouth.

JON WEECE, *Jesus Prom*

Snow days were the best. They still are. On one such day, my brother and I zipped up our coats and headed out to play. The snow had been on the ground for a few days. The weather had warmed the previous afternoon, melting the top layer of snow, but it had refrozen over night. The conditions eliminated the possibility of making a snowball.

So I made an iceball, packing it tightly as I snuck around the side of the house.

My stealthy movements went undetected as I gripped a baseball-sized iceball of death. From eighty feet away, I took a bunny hop, planted my foot, and launched the projectile toward my unsuspecting brother.

You may not believe me when I tell you this, but I really did not want to hit him. This is tough to explain, since I looked at him, aimed at him, and chucked the iceball at him. I just wanted to get it close to him, and the best way to get it close was to aim right at him.

What are the chances my missile would find its mark from such a distance?

Boys experience this phenomenon a lot. We like the challenge of the long shot, but we don't really want to break the glass window. As soon as the iceball launched from my hand, the world seemed to go into slow motion. I instantly imagined the projectile locking in to my brother's face like a heat-seeking missile. He suddenly seemed so innocent. *If only I could hit the abort button*, I thought. But it was gone. It was out of my hands.

Smack!

The left side of his face took a direct hit. On the positive side of things, some of the ice stuck to his face, which helped reduce the immediate swelling.[2]

Once you throw an iceball, you can't alter its route. Likewise, you can't undo your spoken words. Once they escape, they can't be recaptured. I've tried to snag the harsh words firing from my lips, but they fly too fast. Damage control becomes my next best option.

> Everyone should be quick to listen, slow to speak and slow
> to become angry, because human anger does not produce the
> righteousness that God desires.
>
> JAMES 1:19-20

The damage done by one word or one action or even one inaction can crash through families, communities, and countries. Devastating aftershocks can be felt for generations. I need to speak less.

> The one who talks much will for sure sin, but he who is careful
> what he says is wise.
>
> PROVERBS 10:19, NLV

Have you ever noticed how the wisest people in the room often speak the least? And when they speak, everyone listens. The great virtue of those who hold their tongues, however, is not slowness of mind. Wisdom travels alongside the person who places filters between their brains and lips. If we peel back the layers of such people, we'll find a precious virtue tucked away: Humility envelops the wise. The humble admit they don't have all of the answers. The humble recognize that their quick wit won't change a heart. The humble handle their instincts with caution. The humble can take a punch, because they desire God's glory over their own. The humble can live with insult, because they don't think of themselves as higher than they are.

Humility assumes we have more to learn than we do to teach. Humility listens. Humility doesn't become angry. Humility thinks of the other before the self. Humility clears a path for truth and peace to be seen and known.

In order for courage to be effective, it must be paired with humility. Without humility and the care that comes with it, our words can be damaging rather than healing. Yesterday, the words that left my mouth packed more harshness than I intended. Ten minutes later, I found my daughter crying in her bed. I wish I would've placed a series of filters between my brain and my tongue.

My wife, Beth, posted a sign on our refrigerator that offers healthy filters for our words:

Before you speak, THINK:
Is it True?
Is it Helpful?
Is it Inspiring?
Is it Necessary?
Is it Kind?

Yes, there are times when we need to speak more. We'll talk about those situations shortly, but let's begin here. It's what most of us need to hear and apply. Speak wise words to the world, but you probably need to begin by speaking less and listening more.

// REVENGE-LESS

It seems as if every good Western flick features a cowboy with an itchy trigger finger and a score to settle. His "shoot first and ask questions later" bravado leaves a constant stream of messes for his sidekick to clean up. The saloon requires a new window, the sheriff demands a promise of no more troublemaking, the bystander deserves an apology, and the rival gang plots their own revenge.

I've seen families caught in endless cycles of revenge. They may feel bad for causing damage, but they don't break the cycle. They become so comfortable with damage control that they become comfortable with causing damage. We all need to be quick to make amends, but we also need to change our behavior that keeps forcing us to make amends.

I once met with a feuding couple and quickly realized that their past wounds were still infected. The husband had told the wife she was a lazy mom. He later apologized, bought flowers, and affirmed her as a mother, but guess what she unloaded as we talked? His biting words were still biting. And her revengeful biting words to him were still biting him.

You know what's better than mending a broken arm? Not breaking an arm.

You know what's better than damage control? Not needing to do damage control.

You know what's better than apologizing for being a jerk? Not being a jerk.

We need the humility to admit that our first response might be a bad one, and we need the rare courage to walk away from a fight.

> Starting a quarrel is like breaching a dam;
>> so drop the matter before a dispute breaks out.
> PROVERBS 17:14

Jackie Robinson, the first African American to play major league baseball, demonstrated uncanny courage and humility by subduing his instincts to lash out at racist players, fans, and coaches. He was mocked, belittled, and threatened. Pitchers hurled fastballs at his head, and agitators insulted his wife. Anger swelled in his heart, but he knew lashing out would forfeit the greater cause—including and accepting all people. Retaliation would thwart progress. Racism on both sides would have dug deeper into the bunkers. Or dugouts, as the case may be.

In the recent movie about Jackie's life, one of my favorite dialogues occurs between Robinson and the Brooklyn Dodgers' owner, Branch Rickey. Rickey demanded that Robinson bite his tongue and relax his fist, even when tormented with slurs and threats. Doing so would be no small task. Stunned by Rickey's order, Robinson protested:

"You want a player who doesn't have the guts to fight back?"

Rickey: "No, I want a player who's got the guts *not* to fight back."

Robinson: "Give me a uniform . . . give me a number on my back . . . and I'll give you the guts."[3]

Robinson did just that. The color barrier in baseball was pummeled. Robinson's brave humility changed the game, but more importantly, it changed hearts.

If we added application to Romans 12:3, it might read, "Do not think of yourself [or your career, looks, accomplishments, education, athleticism, ideas, or opinions] more highly than you ought." We lay all those things down at the feet of Jesus, and it feels as if we're giving away all we have. For a moment. Then God shows us that what we laid down was never ours to keep in the first place. Robinson laid down revenge. Only the courageous and humble can sacrifice their plans of revenge.

Sometimes I have imaginary conversations with people who've made me mad. You wouldn't believe how well I put them in their lowly place. I look like a hero. Sometimes I repeat the same dominating argument over and over again. If you could see what happens in my brain, you'd think I was really awesome. Or maybe you'd see the truth: I have issues.

Novelist Charles Johnson, in his fictional book on Martin Luther King Jr.'s life, *Dreamer*, re-creates a real sermon preached after King and others had been assaulted in Chicago. In Johnson's book, King says,

> Every night when I get down on my knees to pray or close
> my eyes in quiet meditation I'm holding a funeral for the
> self. I'm digging a little grave for the ego. I'm saying, like the
> lovely Catholic nun I read about who works with the poor in
> Calcutta, that I will despoil myself of all that is not God; I will
> strip my heart of every created thing; I will live in poverty

and detachment; I will renounce my will, my inclinations, my whims and fancies, and make myself a willing servant of the will of God.[4]

Courage and humility demand we sacrifice many of our words and our lust for revenge. But as Chuck Thomas discovered, sometimes they'll also demand we stand up and speak. Sometimes God calls us to speak bravely on his behalf.

ROOSTERS NEEDED

Peter was the man. He was a pillar of the early church, one of the three people closest to Jesus, a leader, an authority, and a powerful preacher. Peter carried a great amount of clout. But Peter had blown it before, and Galatians 2 tells us how he blew it again. This time, there were no roosters to remind him of his sin.

Peter, along with Paul, James, and others, crafted the church's position on Gentile inclusion. Acts 15 details how they concluded that Gentiles did not have to become Jews in order to be Christians. Peter accepted this truth from Christ. In fact, he was enjoying the lightened dietary restrictions. The church was thriving, as Jews and Gentiles alike came to Christ.

That's when the hardliners showed up. Mired in prejudice, they kept their distance from the Gentiles. And in Peter's mind, these hardliners were the cool kids. Peter followed their lead and withdrew from the Gentiles too.

Don't underestimate the hurt caused by Peter's sin. Imagine if you were a Gentile Christian in this day. You have been overjoyed that the gospel has come to you. You have been celebrating your freedom and hope in Jesus and savoring the sweetness of deep fellowship and friendship. And then Peter turns his back on you. The message he communicates is that when push comes to shove, you are still in opposing bunkers. You are an outsider. The promises of Christ are not really for you after all.

Peter's actions threatened to destroy the church. The implications were eternal.

No rooster was around to bring Peter to his senses—but Paul was.

When people start driving others into bunkers, truth and peace are in jeopardy. So waste no time. Act and speak.

We remain ignorant of many of the details about their encounter, but Paul's confrontation of Peter was vocal enough to be heard by Peter's fellow offenders. Paul gave Peter a verbal spanking, but his motive was reconciliation. His words took courage, but his motive took humility.

Paul went where we are called to go: into the fray, into no man's land, disarming those who would destroy one another. Galatians 2:20 has always been one of my favorite verses, but it wasn't until recently that I realized its connection to this story. Paul admonished Peter,

If I rebuild what I destroyed, then I really would be a lawbreaker. . . . I have been crucified with Christ and I no longer live, but Christ lives in me.

GALATIANS 2:18-20

Peter had begun rebuilding the walls of prejudice that were stiff-arming people away from the gospel. He was rebuilding what the church had toiled to destroy.

Paul then reminded Peter of how he could bring peace to a fractured world. Christ makes possible human impossibilities: "I no longer live, but Christ lives in me." Christ replaces my prejudice with peace, my hurtful barbs with healing words, and my revenge with restoration.

If you view yourself as more important than others, or if your fears are bigger than your convictions, you'll stay stuck in your bunker. Courage without humility is just arrogance. But when the two come together, not only can we climb out of our bunkers, but we can also take others with us.

This world needs more people like Paul and my friend Chuck. Their courage was rooted in humility. They were brave for the sake of God's Kingdom, not for their own glory. We desperately need people to confront wrongdoing. We need people with the courage to quit defending their crooked politician, company, or kid. We need people of integrity and sincerity. We need people of good standing. We need people willing to sweat and toil for the sake of peacemaking. We need you to take courage, step into no man's land, and compel others to do the same.

REFLECTION QUESTIONS

1. Is it easier for you to be courageous or humble?

2. What are you tempted to consider more highly than you ought (Romans 12:3)? Your career, education, ideas, looks?

3. When have you seen someone, like Chuck Thomas, bring peace to a divisive situation?

4. When are you apt to speak too much? How can you begin listening in this situation?

5. Pray about any divisive issue in your sphere of influence. Is God calling you to act?

PART III

PATHS TO FREEDOM

Steve Trevor: This is no man's land, Diana! It means no man can cross it, alright? This battalion has been here for nearly a year and they've barely gained an inch. . . .

Diana Prince (Wonder Woman): So . . . what? So we do nothing?

Steve Trevor: . . . We can't save everyone in this war. This is not what we came here to do.

Diana Prince: No. But it's what I'm going to do.

Wonder Woman, 2017

CHAPTER 13

THE WAY THROUGH

No matter how much we wanted to be out of the minefield, the rule was never rush, take your time. . . . "Once you make a false step, a hundred lifetimes cannot redeem it."[1]

IN AUGUST OF 1961, the German Democratic Republic (East Germany) built a wall. The wall's job was not to protect but to imprison. Residents were told that death awaited anyone trying to escape. Three days later, the first person tried. Many more would attempt the same.

Ingo Bethke was one of the victims trapped behind the Berlin Wall. He was the son of hard-line communists, but the twenty-one-year-old longed for freedom and adventure.

On May 22, 1975, just before midnight, Ingo and a friend set off on a daring flight to freedom. Soldiers, a stretch of land called the death strip, and the River Elbe stood in their way.

They nonchalantly walked right past two soldiers. The soldiers never noticed the bulge below Ingo's arm, which was a deflated blow-up mattress. They'd passed their first test, but the worst was yet to come.

Hazards littered the death strip. First, he and his friend treaded through a strip of sand that had been carefully raked to detect footprints.

Next, a menacing fence of metal, barbed wire, and trip wire blocked their path. However, Ingo had managed to cut a hole in one portion of the fence during one of his earlier patrols. They found it and slipped through undetected.

Behind the fence was an area littered with mines. Ingo maneuvered the minefield by using a long wooden block to check the ground in front of them. Ingo held his breath and prodded the ground in front of him with the plank, praying his next step would not be his last. Prayer after prayer was answered.

After navigating the minefield, they crawled to the river's edge and inflated the air mattress as a makeshift raft. Police boats with spotlights patrolled the river, but a thick fog obscured their view. Climbing into the water, they paddled as quickly but quietly as they could. Thirty minutes later they reached land.

An officer in some type of border police van spotted the shivering, dripping friends. "It's a cold night for swimming," the officer said with a smile.

"Not when you're swimming out of the East," Ingo said, grinning.[2] They'd made it to Lower Saxony, the West . . . freedom.

FINDING FREEDOM

As we look around us, it may feel as though our culture, our churches, even our closest relationships are full of minefields. No man's land might sound nice, but why risk it when you're sure to set off an explosion no matter where you step?

It often seems impossible to get beyond racial divides. I just finished reading *Between the World and Me* by Ta-Nehisi Coates.[3] The book is brilliant, poetic, and eye-opening. And it also left me feeling hopeless. He concludes that the best his son can do is to struggle in a losing battle. In some ways, I can't blame him. Anger, ignorance, distrust, and hurt flow through our conversations about race. Coates doesn't believe in God, so he doesn't believe in the impossible or the power of Christ to overhaul a heart. I do, so I refuse to lose all hope. I'll keep searching for paths forward.

Our political climate seems full of fury and division. You're wrong if you're not in the "right" party or the "left." Everyone seems to be looking out for their own interests and trying to yell over the top of each other. Our walls go up and our bunkers go deep. If God cares about us, he cares about how we participate in politics.

Class warfare dogs most communities. Just this past week, I heard an affluent woman thumb her nose at the people from "that part of town" (which happened to be my part of town), and I got cussed at by a man whose request for money was denied by our church (even though we'd helped him before). Jesus rubbed shoulders with the elites and the outcasts, so there's hope for us to learn some paths forward with diverse social classes.

Generational discord is frequently overlooked as a major problem in our country, but the results are tragic. God loves all people, young and old, so we need to find paths forward to do the same.

And no divisions in our world grieve God more than those he sees in the church, his body. When we use faith as an excuse to build bunkers, everyone gets hurt: churched and unchurched alike. The Bible has a ton to say about Christian unity, so we'll be well equipped to clear the brush from our path. I hope we'll have the will to move forward.

As we know, these are not the only minefields around us. Wherever we look, cultural flash points are causing people to dive into bunkers. We can't tackle every issue in this book, but the attitudes and actions that lead us into no man's land are going to provide a template for facing any divisive issue. Where some people see only minefields, we can find a path to freedom. Traversing to peace may require you to step by explosive issues and tense, weapon-bearing guards. Fear will tempt you to retreat into complacency. Complacency will invite you to huddle with its friends. You'll be reminded that you cannot instantly bring truth and peace to every volatile situation. But you can still march on.

The path to freedom is difficult but worth the journey. You can bring healing, calmness, and clarity to your family, workplace, community, and world. I believe that! Do you?

In each of these minefields, we'll proceed with purpose and

discernment. Wisdom and love. Truth and peace. Both/and. These issues are dividing our nation, churches, communities, and families, so if we want to step into no man's land, if we truly want to find freedom, we must weigh our response carefully. And our response will include action. Each of the chapters includes application for individuals and groups. I'm especially hopeful that church leaders will pay close attention, because I believe churches can lead the way.

There is a good path out of the bunkers and into no man's land, no matter how dangerous the minefield. The path is messy and tough, but we'll seek to find and navigate it together.

REFLECTION QUESTIONS

1. Are you more apt to freeze with fear or charge carelessly ahead?

2. Which of the issues we'll discuss causes you the most stress?

3. What helps you paddle both quickly and cautiously?

4. Are you willing to humbly self-examine your heart and explore the "paths to freedom" related to these topics?

5. Ask God to teach you how to navigate the specific issues we're about to explore.

CHAPTER 14

DIVIDED DIVERSITY

Speak justice. Do justice. Forgive the unjust. That's the way of Christ. No way around it.

CARLOS A. RODRÍGUEZ

ON JUNE 17, 2015, a small group of people gathered in the Emanuel African Methodist Episcopal Church in downtown Charleston, South Carolina. The historic church had served as a pillar of the African American community in Charleston for two centuries. On that Wednesday night, they came together to study their Bibles and pray. When a young man named Dylann Roof entered the church, they welcomed him warmly. He listened and even participated in the discussion for about an hour, but the group's kindness could not penetrate his cold heart. Suddenly, Roof pulled out a gun and began to spew racist threats at the group. Twenty-six-year-old Tywanza Sanders quickly tried to intervene, speaking calmly to Roof. But the hate that coursed through Roof's soul squeezed the trigger. And again. And again. And again. And again . . .[1]

Nine innocent Christians were slain that night by a person who acted on a deep-seated hatred of people with a different skin color—a hatred so deep-seated that he carried the symbols of apartheid Rhodesia and South Africa, as well as the slavery-based Confederacy.

A century and a half after the abolition of slavery and half a century after the Civil Rights Act, racial strife still plagues our country. Some people note how things are better today than they were fifty years ago. In many ways, they are right. Many lives were given for the sake of equality. Others note how America was born with the racism of slavery, and the curse keeps rearing its ugly head. In many ways, they are right too. In my city, the largely African American population of North Tulsa has an average lifespan of ten years less than the rest of the city. You can list a dozen reasons why this is, but you can't pretend the curse of racism has been completely erased.

Bunkers have been built with extreme positions. People blame the other side for every ill, and the gap between the two grows. It feels as if we are forced to make a tiresome choice between two nonexistent Americas: one that is irretrievably and unforgivably racist, and another where there is no racism, discrimination, or privilege at all.

SKIN DEEP

About three thousand years ago, God sent the prophet Samuel to anoint the next king of Israel, whom God said was at the house of Jesse. When Jesse brought out Eliab, his tall, handsome firstborn son, Samuel was confident he had his man: "Surely I'm looking at the next king of Israel." But God had his eyes on the youngest son, a lowly shepherd boy named David. God revealed a timeless truth to Samuel that day: "People look at the outward appearance, but the LORD looks at the heart" (1 Samuel 16:7).

We usually focus on the second truth in that sentence, and I'm glad. It teaches us about God's beautiful character. But let's not rush past the first part of the verse: "People look at the outward appearance." Seeing how God colorfully and beautifully created the human race is wonderful. The problem God identified was that people are prone to make snap, preju-dicial judgments based on what they see. Samuel wrongly assumed that a king must have a certain look. Thousands of years later, the human race is still plagued by our inclination to judge people based on their looks. And sometimes *judging* is the same as *hating*.

Earlier I told you that you can't love me and hate my children. If you hate them, you hate me, no matter what you say. God feels the same, so let me press the illustration a little further.

One of my daughters is African American. The rule about hating my children still applies with her. So the church member who told me, "Blacks are lazy" insulted me. I asked him, "Are you saying my girl is lazy?" He tried to backtrack and say how she might not be like that. I didn't want to pick a fight, but I also wanted him to know that he'd been very hurtful. He'd insulted everyone who looked like my daughter. He'd equated skin color with character.

It hurts me when someone I know makes a statement like this, but it also hurts me when my friends don't rebuke or correct those kinds of statements. I want you to know that if you are complicit with these kinds of comments, you're insulting me. Has it ever occurred to you that people might say these things to you because they think you agree with them? You can't love me and quietly agree with those who trash-talk my girl.

I'm not asking you to cuss at the next guy who makes a stupid comment. That would undo everything we've been learning. But I do think God expects us to exhibit discernment, courage, and shrewdness, while still bathing them in gentleness and humility.

I've not experienced the kind of prejudice that many of you know all too well. I wanted to learn from someone who endured violent prejudice, but instead of seeking revenge found a path toward forgiveness, hope, and freedom. And I found a wise teacher in one of the most respected people in our country.

THE HOPE

The quiet clatter of spoons on soup bowls fills the café, but all of it is only backdrop for the intense, deliberate voice of Dr. John Perkins.

When Dr. Perkins speaks about reconciliation, he can't sit still. As he and I talk, he sways back and forth and then leans in close to emphasize a particular axiom or piece of Scripture. John Perkins is generous with his time and has a relentless commitment to investing his wisdom and kindness into the lives of others.

People know Dr. Perkins for many things. Many identify him as a man who cares deeply about the dream of Martin Luther King Jr. Others note his groundbreaking work to help people rise from poverty. Still others mention his dedication to family. But to really understand Dr. Perkins, you must know one thing: The gospel changed his life.[2]

John Perkins was born into a Mississippi family of sharecroppers and bootleggers. After his father abandoned them, his mother and siblings fended for themselves in a system where they'd never have enough and would never be able to improve their situation. Perkins couldn't even enjoy the luxury of a grade-school education—how could he go to school when his family needed him in the cotton field?

The more he experienced mistreatment and witnessed the oppression of his situation, the angrier Perkins grew. The final straw came when his older brother, shortly after returning from World War II, was murdered by a racist cop in the town square. Perkins held his brother, his hero, as his life bled away in the back seat of a car. Fearful that Perkins would share his brother's fate, the family sent him to California to live with a relative.

Life steadied. He found employment, housing, friends, and a more peaceful existence. During a visit back to Mississippi, he also found his wife, Vera Mae, who moved to California with him. He refers to her as God's great gift to him. Perkins excelled in his work, their family grew, and they never intended to return to Mississippi.

That's when God stepped in. Through the encouragement of his young son and a local church, Perkins heard about God's love for all people. *All people.* He'd never really grasped this truth before. Soon he committed his life to Christ, asking Jesus to forgive his sins and heal his wounds. He also felt called by God to do good work. He and Vera Mae plunged themselves into leading Bible studies, volunteering with the church, and caring for neighborhood kids. Life was good—and yet,

God began nudging them to return to Mississippi. The needs near their hometown were immense. John and Vera Mae understood that opposition awaited, but they chose obedience. With the support of Christian friends in California, they returned to the South.

Perkins believes in ministry that leads to wholeness in individuals, families, and communities. In the South, he sensed that wholeness would require both mercy and justice. People in the community had immense needs—spiritual, physical, educational, medical, economic, and systematic. And so, following the call to offer mercy, Dr. Perkins began laying the groundwork for what is now called the Christian Community Development Association,[3] which has trained thousands and blessed hundreds of thousands or more.

But Dr. Perkins knew that he could not express mercy without risking the dangers of pursuing justice. He understood the brutal, systematic injustice that deprived African Americans of opportunity and hope. African Americans made up 31 percent of the population, yet not one had ever been granted a municipal job. African Americans were not paid even the minimum wage. Federal laws were ignored. Unwarranted arrests were common. Health care denied. Voting blocked. Education sabotaged. Housing discriminated. And guess which was the only part of town without paved streets?

In the South, control was the name of the game. So when the consistent discrimination and lack of power to change it backed Perkins into a corner, he led his fellow African Americans in a boycott. Economic pressure was a way to exert some control. Their peaceful, nonviolent protest landed a heavy blow. Those in power were furious. The "haves" would not stand idly by while the "have-nots" threatened their comfort.

On February 7, 1970, police ambushed Dr. Perkins and his peaceful friends. They were arrested without cause, tortured, and beaten almost to death in a Mississippi jail. At one point during the night, his friends were sure life had left John's motionless body. In that moment, God taught him what he believes is the greatest lesson he's ever learned.

At this point in his story to me, he sat up in his chair, glanced around the room, locked his eyes back on mine, and then leaned in close.

I thought I was going to die in that jail. My friends thought I was already dead. I guess I looked like it. When I came back to consciousness, [the police officers] beat me some more. In the midst of the beatings, hate filled my heart. If I could've pushed a button to make a bomb explode in that room, I would've done it. If I could've grabbed a grenade, I would've pulled the pin and dropped it. I would've killed those men.

In the darkness of that moment, I realized my evil matched theirs. They wanted to kill me, and I wanted to kill them. The only difference was that they had the means to do it. I deserved hell, just like them. I was the worst of sinners. Because I hated those racist cops, they were victims too. We were both victims, because we hated and were hated. There are two victims in every failed relationship.

Once we see our own depravity, we can hear grace and truth. John Newton [who penned "Amazing Grace"] admitted his own sin after hearing the misery of the slaves. He needed forgiveness from God first, and then he could ask forgiveness from others. My heart was broken in that Mississippi jail. I knew the only way I could help people was if God changed my heart.[4]

Perkins believes that Galatians 2:20 is at the heart of any productive reconciliation effort: "I have been crucified with Christ and I no longer live, but Christ lives in me." Unless we put to death the sin and hate in our own hearts, and unless we let Christ take the reins of our thoughts, feelings, and actions, reconciliation doesn't have a chance. Reconciliation begins with your heart and with mine. Perkins continued,

Hate is ingrained in us. We have to let God ingrain love in us, and that only happens through finding our core identification with Christ. Hitler was Arian-centric. Idi Amin was Afro-centric. "Centric" has to go. We can only be Christ-centric.[5]

Before you start feeling completely removed from the problem, recognize that *self-centric* is no better than *Arian-centric*. Arian-centrists are, after all, Arian. Whom does the Arian-centrists' worldview benefit? Them*selves*! Anne Lamott wrote, "You can safely assume you've created God in your own image when it turns out that God hates all the same people you do."[6]

Some claim Christianity is intolerant, but Martin Luther King Jr. believed progress completely depended upon the culture's Christ-centeredness and submission to One Absolute Authority: "In contrast to the ethical relativism of Communism, Christianity sets forth a system of absolute moral values and affirms that God has placed within the very structure of this universe certain moral principles that are fixed and immutable."[7]

Civil rights are crippled without an Absolute Authority to determine what is ultimately right or wrong. If we can humbly submit to Christ as our center, we can move toward justice and love and away from hate and silence.

John Piper hopefully daydreams, "Imagine what race relations and racial controversies would look like if the participants were all dead to pride and deeply humble before God and each other."[8]

RECONCILIATION

God was reconciling the world to himself in Christ, not counting people's sins against them. And he has committed to us the message of reconciliation. We are therefore Christ's ambassadors, as though God were making his appeal through us.

2 CORINTHIANS 5:19-20

Reconciliation can be defined as the restoration of a damaged relationship. Our sin separates us from God, but Christ's death on the cross pays for our sin. Christ became sin, so that we can be reconciled to God. In the most precious of acts, he restores our damaged relationship.

That's not all. God calls us to be ministers of reconciliation, helping others find peace with God. We march together with God in his great mission, bringing sinners from every culture to salvation.

And we reconcile people not only vertically (to God), but also horizontally (to each other). A husband can be reconciled to his wife. A daughter can be reconciled to her father. A wounded student can be reconciled to her friend. And whole people groups can be reconciled to others. If you are a Christian, you have the grand privilege and crystal-clear command of reconciling people to God and each other. From Jesus' encounter with the "racially despised" Samaritan woman . . . to his lengthy prayer for unity . . . to the first church intentionally breaking ethnic, cultural, and economic barriers, the biblical mandate stands tall.[9] Paul revealed this great mystery in his letter to the Ephesians: Even Gentiles can be reconciled to God.

Christian work shatters cultural divides: "There is neither Jew nor Gentile, neither slave nor free, nor is there male and female, for you are all one in Christ Jesus."[10] The early church worked tirelessly to reconcile these listed groups to God and to each other, a massive and worthy undertaking. Their work was not without controversy, conflict, or confrontation. But they pressed on. And so must we.

Perhaps a modern translation of Galatians would read, "There is neither African nor European, neither rich nor poor, neither old nor young, neither Republican nor Democrat, for you are all one in Christ Jesus." While we participate in and can be grateful for our particular identities, cultures, upbringings, and ethnicities, we never celebrate them above our identity in Christ.

Does that bother you? If so, your hopes of reconciliation will drown in pride. But if you embrace your identity in Christ, reconciliation breaks through. Be intentional in the work of reconciliation.

// 1. ENCOURAGE ONE ANOTHER

Not long ago, my home city, Tulsa, was the scene of a police shooting. Tears flowed, tensions grew, and the media descended upon us. Opposing narratives were written, each painting their side as angelic and the other as demonic:

- *He had it coming. He should've followed orders.*
- *He was totally innocent. He was never a threat.*
- *The shooting was racially motivated. If he was white, he'd still be alive.*
- *The shooting was warranted. She (the police officer) was just doing her job.*

"Jump into our bunker or you are our enemy," we could hear them yell. It felt as if we were building toward an explosion.

A few days after the shooting, the word *encourage* came to mind. I drove to the church of an African American preacher friend of mine. His church is near where the shooting occurred. I figured some of his church members knew the deceased, Terence Crutcher, so it was even more traumatic for them. However, my friend wasn't there. I thought of driving home, but I felt even more compelled to find someone to encourage. I saw another church building down the street, so I decided to introduce myself. My knocks were answered by the pastor of the church, who cautiously opened the door. Their church van had been vandalized the night before. She'd come to check on things and had then decided to stay and pray for the people of their church. I told her I'd come to offer encouragement and prayer. If you looked at Faye Martinez and me, you might notice our differences, but by the time I left that morning, she was my friend. Two days later, I joined her and other pastors near her neighborhood to pray for the city. We continue to meet weekly.

The next day, I was scarfing an oversize sandwich at Quiznos when a police officer walked in. The word *pay* came to mind. Just as Mr. Crutcher's community suffered, so, too, did our law enforcement officers. It was a terrible time for them. I jumped back in line to pay for his meal, and then I assured him of our church's care for him, our law officers, and our city.

Many Tulsans refused to join either of the opposing bunkers. African American church leaders and city officials worked harmoniously to promote healing, peace, and justice. And while working with each other, they absorbed shots from those who remained in bunkers. Diverse friendships had already been established, and trust and hope won the day. We're praying that progress continues.

If you have an opportunity to contribute to the national dialogue today, take it. But if you don't, find someone to love and encourage. Sweeten the day of someone different from you, and if enough of us do this over and over again, perhaps we'll accomplish more than we ever thought we could. As Paul says in Galatians, "Let us not become weary in doing good, for at the proper time we will reap a harvest if we do not give up" (6:9).

// 2. LISTEN

We've highlighted the value of listening already in this book, but it warrants one last mention here. I can't think of another issue that shuts down listening any quicker than this one. In cartoons, steam comes out of the ears of irate people. In real life, the steam may not come out of our ears, but it at least clogs them. Emotionally charged people can't hear a thing.

The other day, I was talking to a friend who was riled up about a group of people. He complained about how their "issues" were all blown out of proportion by the media. I asked him if he'd talked to anyone from that group of people, and he admitted he had not. Guess who had framed his opinion? The media!

Please don't be that guy. You have my permission, and encouragement, to ignore the voices from the edges—often the media, bloggers, and irate people. But listen to people with different perspectives and opinions than yours. Then and only then should you begin to form an opinion.

Nate Pyle wrote, "To understand racism you need to understand power dynamics. To understand sexism you need to understand power dynamics. To understand poverty you need to understand power dynamics. To understand power dynamics you need to listen and believe the stories of the powerless."[11] We still use discernment, but we can't expect any improvement if we dismiss everything that contradicts—or simply adds perspective to—our own experience.

Recently a lot of Americans were arguing about a movement to remove a Confederate statue from a public park. (And regardless of your opinion, can we still be friends, please?) I had a friend who posted on social media that he was tired of the politically correct crowd removing memorials erected to honor fallen soldiers shortly after the Civil War. But an amazing thing happened: He listened and learned. He later posted on social media that he'd learned many of the statues (and specifically, the ones closest to his town) had not been erected after the war to honor the fallen. They'd been erected at the height of Jim Crow as a means to intimidate African Americans. Some of the speeches made by city officials during the statues' unveiling revealed their intentions. For my friend, this knowledge didn't make him hell-bent on tearing down every relic in the country but instead moved him to a more nuanced position. What encouraged me was that he was able to listen, learn, and show the humility to change his mind. In the end, he was closer to truth and peace than he was before. The path forward for us requires lots of listening and learning.

// 3. BE GRACIOUS

Be wise in the way you act toward outsiders; make the most of every opportunity. Let your conversation be always full of grace, seasoned with salt, so that you may know how to answer everyone.
COLOSSIANS 4:5-6

In this passage, Paul addresses the way Christians should interact with unbelievers, and it's a perfect template for your interaction with anyone different from you.

1. *Make the best use of your time.* Wouldn't listening to a friend with a different cultural background be a better use of time than listening to a talk radio host who gets paid to rally his base (otherwise known as his bunker)?
2. *Speak graciously.* We get so offended so quickly. Brant Hansen wrote a book called *Unoffendable.* He makes a compelling case

that the only reason we're entitled to get offended or live angry is if we've never offended anyone else. Wow, that really narrows down the possibilities, doesn't it? We can't enter this discussion while waving our offenses. To have a conversation about race, you'll need lots of grace. Allow for some awkwardness. Let each other misspeak a time or two. Correct a bad assumption or stereotype, but don't cut off the relationship. I like the picture of using one of those huge cheese dispensers (like they use at Olive Garden for your salad) to sprinkle grace all over a diverse group of friends. Be gracious; then we'll move past the awkward and get to the really good stuff.

// 4. PRACTICE HOSPITALITY

A common denominator unites the previous three practical steps: relationships required. You can't encourage, speak graciously to, or listen to someone unless you are with them—I mean *really* with them. Don't trade a real conversation for an argument in the comment section of an online newspaper.

> Above all, love each other deeply, because love covers over a multitude of sins. Offer hospitality to one another without grumbling. Each of you should use whatever gift you have received to serve others, as faithful stewards of God's grace in its various forms.
>
> I PETER 4:8-10

There's something beautiful, vulnerable, even spiritual about inviting others to your table. You serve, you laugh, you pray, you care. My friend Sean Palmer once gave his church a summer challenge: "Invite someone different from you to your home for a meal. Then ask them about their perspective. Then shut up." His church learned to be with others, listen to others, encourage others. Lots of gracious conversations occurred that summer.

Some of you will have to be intentional about forging diverse friendships. So be intentional. Pray and make an effort. The opportunities for diverse friendships in your town may be different from mine, and that's okay. Do what you can, share a meal, and God will do beautiful things in your path forward.

WHERE IS THE CHURCH?

My friend Steve Chapman persistently asks, "Is the American church doing enough?"

At her best, the church led the way in the development of social views about race. However, at other times the church has written itself into the background as race issues persist. Where was the church during the 1870s when the immediate advancements of the Civil War were lost to passage of southern Jim Crow laws, the establishment of new laws that essentially returned former slaves to the oppression of the plantation? Where was the church during the terrorism of the Ku-Klux-Klan in the late nineteenth and much of the twentieth century? Where was the church when we imprisoned our citizens of Japanese descent in WWII internment camps? Where was the church in the 1940s and 50s when the GI-Bill ushered in another era of segregated housing? Where was the church when police brutality nearly ended the life of Dr. Perkins? Where was the church when entire communities crumbled in the wake of economic, educational, medical, and judicial disadvantage? How has the church offered her voice to address the issues of ethnic poverty since the war on poverty was waged? Worse yet, why did historically white churches abandon ethnically changing neighborhoods in the urban centers, instead of finding ways to minister to the changing face of their community?

The United States has had a festering catastrophe since the rise of African enslavement to cultivate the plantations in the southern colonies. Naively, many in the church have accepted a narrative that claims the "racial" problems have been solved, if not by the North's victory in the "war between the states," then by the civil rights activities of the 60s. But when a young man walked into an African-American church to ruthlessly murder its members, only because their melanin levels were higher than his own, some people were rocked from their slumber. It is time for Christians to redeem a narrative that moves us from prejudice to harmony![12]

Martin Luther King Jr. lamented that Sunday morning was the most segregated hour in America. We can blame many factors, but any of those reflections will be fruitless unless we first reject the presumption that "it's the way things will always be; some things can't change."

CHURCH STEPS

Most church leaders could sincerely tell you their doors stand wide open for anyone to enter. But a statement like that demands a follow-up question: "If your doors are open to everybody, why is there no diversity in your church?" Church leaders who bristle at the mention of diversity, regardless of the reason, all have one thing in common: no diversity.

One steamy August afternoon at a leadership retreat, our church elders, after a season of Bible study and prayer, looked each other in the eye and declared, "We value diversity, it brings glory to God, and it helps us obey the great commission. We must pursue it." That unified resolve from our elders marked a new chapter in our church's life.

When we speak about diversity with our church, we always tell people why we value it. We desire to be multiethnic, multigenerational, and socioeconomically diverse. We seek not political correctness but obedience to God. We want to see peace in our hearts, our streets, and our world. We've taken many small steps to remove blinders, obstacles, and misunderstandings.[13] As our church's blog states, "we have a million miles to go," but God has blessed our commitment.

On the Sunday following the Charleston shooting, I stood in front of our church and told them that we weep and pray for our brothers and sisters in South Carolina. The tragedy confirmed why the work of reconciliation is so important. I told them that if the shooter would've grown up in a diverse church, full of love and friendship, he never could've pulled the trigger. He would've heard about God's heart for all people, and he would've known and loved people who looked different from him. He would've broken free from the inherited prejudices that stoked his hate.

If your church is blessed enough to be in a diverse community, don't ignore the biblical mandate for reconciliation and don't miss the blessings a diverse church brings. If your church doesn't know where to begin, start with two simple steps:

1. *Expand your relationships.* Invite people with different backgrounds, cultures, or skin tones than yours, and ask them questions about how your church can better serve them. Ask if you accidentally do anything insensitive. Give permission for them to offer continued input. And invite them to be part of your desire to care for all people.
2. *Read helpful books.* I've made a great list in the endnotes.[14]

I once heard a sports commentator talking about how the success of both the Kansas City Royals and the Kansas City Chiefs had united their city. I wanted to cry. If our hopes for unity rest upon the shoulders of the Chiefs (who crush my heart with a devastating loss every year in the playoffs), we're toast. The church, not a sports team, should lead the way in bringing diverse people into a beautiful mosaic of God's finest art.

PRESS ON

Edward Gilbreath, in his important book *Reconciliation Blues*, tells of a meeting he attended in 2005.[15] A group of about fifty leaders, all of them esteemed in the work of reconciliation, gathered in Indianapolis.

Although Gilbreath anticipated the gathering with excitement, his buzz quickly evaporated as leader after leader lamented the lack of progress in their communities. The meeting felt like a funeral. He noted, "An impulsive reaction for Christians immersed in the work of social justice and reconciliation is to become flustered, angry or bitter even as they trudge along in their ministries." Concerns increased about how the meeting would conclude. Would they all leave with nothing but discouragement?

The answer came toward the end of the day, when Dr. Perkins suddenly walked into the room. Everyone knew all about Perkins. Gilbreath noted that he was dubbed "the godfather of racial reconciliation."

> Dr. Perkins stood in the middle of the circle, with all eyes fixed upon him. At seventy-five he seemed a little slower than usual but still full of personality. His face, with its strong brown features, was accented by the lines of time. What would he tell us? What wisdom could he, the patriarch of the movement, impart to us on staying the course and fighting the good fight? Gathering his thoughts, he looked at us with a gentle but fierce gaze.

Gilbreath describes how Perkins's fierce gaze gave way to tears. Perkins recounted the suffering he'd endured, but then reminded them of their call:

> "What is God telling us?" Dr. Perkins continued. "I feel he's telling us Philippians 1:6—'He who has begun this good work in you will carry it on to completion until the day of Christ Jesus.' It is God who gave us this ministry, and he will be the one to fulfill it. We just need to continue to give our hearts and souls to loving others and living the gospel in an incarnational way, and then trust God to bring the change."[16]

In five instances in the book of Revelation, John used a familiar phrase to indicate who will be in eternity: "every tribe and language and people and nation."[17] How did John, who saw this vision, know they were from every tribe and language and people and nation? I assume he noted their looks. The church's goal is to be not color-blind but colorful.

I can't wait to be part of that cosmic, diverse worship service. There will be no more hate, divisions, or racial baggage. God will wipe that away, and we'll stand as equal brothers and sisters before our King.

Until that time, let's commit to walking together. I can't be colorful in a bunker by myself. Neither can you. So let's walk together, you and me. Let's invite other neighborhoods, other tribes, other tongues, and other nations on this path to freedom, truth, and peace.

REFLECTION QUESTIONS

1. Do you encourage others in their genuine efforts to bring about reconciliation, even if there are a few flaws in their steps?

2. About whom are you inclined to make snap, prejudiced judgments based on how they look?

3. Are you willing to

   a. Initiate friendships with people different from you?

   b. Speak out against prejudice, just as Paul rebuked and restored Peter (Galatians 2)?

4. How could your church become a healing agent in your community?

5. Which of the four steps do you need to next take (encourage one another, listen, be gracious, or practice hospitality)? Pray about how you'll take this step.

CHAPTER 15

POLITICAL MAYHEM

What have you done to the world, politician? You separate brother from brother like a magician.

JON GIBSON, "METAL MACHINE"

REMEMBER THE ONE TIME YOU regrettably veered a dinner conversation to politics? Now you know better, right? At once, all decency, friendship, and respect were forgotten. And why wouldn't they be? This is *politics* we're talking about. The old joke "*poli* means *many*, and *tics* means *blood-sucking parasites*" works every time.

The word itself has been hijacked to refer to the ideologies of Republicans or Democrats (or other political parties/movements). I prefer a more robust definition: "the way of the people." It's the system for how people live—rules, freedoms, and all. Politics is a way of thinking and living. Knowing a better definition helps us, but only a bit. We're still left fighting over how local and national governments should operate, which laws they should pass, and how we should engage. So for the purposes of this chapter, I'll succumb to the weaker definition of the word. When I speak of politics, I'll be specifically referring to our partisan ideologies of how governments ought to operate.

Politics provides an endless supply of things to fight about. Every day, another story breaks and people argue about it. Too often, we allow our political stances to damage relationships and overrule our convictions. Political issues shouldn't rule us. And we can avoid political bunkers by leaning into the truth of our identity as followers of Christ.

KINGDOM PLAYBOOK

Tony Evans illustrates how politics exposes our true allegiances:

[Football] is the closest thing to an organized gladiator battle in our nation. . . . Yet unlike most battles and unlike most wars, a third team is in this conflict. Three teams take to the field. . . .

Maybe you have never noticed that three teams are on the football field. But I guarantee that you would have noticed if the third team hadn't shown up. Because without this third team, there would be chaos on the field. There would be confusion in the face-off. In fact, there would be no way to play football as we know it.

This is because the third team is the team of officials.

The officials are unique in that their ultimate commitment is not to the teams on the field, nor do they align themselves with any of the other agendas. The officials' obligations do not lie with those who are in the battle, nor even with those watching it take place. Their commitment, as well as their allegiance, belongs to an entirely different kingdom called the NFL office. This kingdom supersedes, overrules, and sits above all others.

From the League office, the officials have been given a book. They have their own book with the governances, guidelines, rules, and regulations by which they are to manage the events on the field. While both teams are constantly pulling at the officials to choose a side, call penalties, or endorse plays, the team of officials must, in spite of personal preferences or emotions, rule according to its kingdom's book. . . .

If at any time an official makes a decision that sides with a team or a particular player—because of pressure from the fans, influence of players or coaching staff, or simply personal preferences—and that does not abide by the book, that official will have immediately lost the support and authority of not only the League office, but also of the commissioner. If the viewpoint of an official ever overrules the viewpoint of the book, superseding the kingdom to which the official is ultimately obligated, the official will no longer rule at all. This is because the NFL headquarters at 345 Park Avenue, New York, New York, will stand by an official only if that official stands by the book. Once an official leaves the book, he has just demoted himself to the status of a fan and become illegitimate in terms of his previously held authority.[1]

As the people of Christ living within the civilizations and cultures of humans, we must look not to the teams around us but to our playbook, the Word of God. But I have to admit that I myself have often worked from an incompatible playbook, replacing God's Word with political, partisan jabber. During my college years, while I was first learning to teach and preach, the delightful people of First Christian Church in Galena, Kansas, allowed me to deliver several sermons for their congregation. I blush when I recall a handful of paragraphs I stupidly jammed into those sermons. To be frank, I wish I had never spoken them aloud.

If you were to read those old handwritten sermon notes, you'd see stretches where I laid aside the objectives of the Kingdom for the objectives of an earthly kingdom. I drifted from the truths of Scripture to the slanted agendas of a political party. I compromised my allegiance to the Kingdom. I'm ashamed of those moments, but I'm forever thankful for a church gracious and instructive enough to mature a novice like me.

As far as I know, in the midst of those ill-fated segments, my intentions were good. That's what makes this subject so slippery. Yes, there are countless political activists with crooked intentions. They look like crooks, smell like crooks, and talk like crooks. But a few steps away from them are millions of people who, while not crooks, completely and wholly believe three ideas:

Their political opinions are well intentioned, even loving.
Their political opinions are logical and proven.
Everyone who disagrees with them is wrong.

Edward Gilbreath writes, "Political bigotry is America's new racism. . . . The two primary colors have morphed from black and white to blue and red—as in 'blue states' [Democrats] and 'red states' [Republicans]."[2] It's why you've heard it said, "I just don't bring up politics anymore." It's why people feel ostracized if they don't toe the party line—the cockamamy rule that says you must pledge blind allegiance to a political party based on your family, religion, ethnicity, or employment.

Referees who care more about a team's playbook than the league rule book will ruin the game, and Christians who care more about their partisan agenda than Christ's agenda will sabotage families, churches, and communities. So, I have to ask, if my knee bows to something or someone other than Christ, am I even a Christian at all?

MEANS TO AN END

An influential faith leader launched an entire campaign to "restore America." An unending stream of his mailers crowd my office mailbox with taglines like "Join me if you think Jesus is the only hope for our country."

Don't get me wrong. I know what he means. He wants America to honor God—a worthy goal indeed. I'm on board. He believes Jesus is the hope for America. Me, too. Sign me up.

But the use of the word *restore* is naive at best and abusive at worst. Shall we restore America to the collective faith that must account for the two hundred years of slavery on its watch? Or one hundred years of Jim Crow laws? Or the sexual revolution? Shall we restore America to the collective faith that must account for Supreme Court decisions that devalued the humanity of African Americans, women, and the unborn? Shall we restore America to a day when life was more palatable for you, regardless of how it tasted to others?

Trust me, I'm concerned for America. We're a mess. Twisted politicians dismay me. The lack of a collective conscience troubles me. Turn on the TV and you'll see a commercial decrying domestic abuse followed by a commercial objectifying women. And we're too distracted to connect the dots.

But here's the deal: Christ followers are no longer following Christ if the restoration of a nation has become their end goal. In much of the promotional material I've received, a subtle but clear objective emerges: *The end goal is a better America, and God will help us get there.* Do you see that? God has become the means for a political end. When has God been okay with being the means to an end?

I won't judge the motives of those behind this campaign, but I can at least hoist the flag of concern. Our country finds itself on a polarized gridiron. Look around and you'll see multiple groups founded on selfish agendas, blinded by fears, wounds, and isolation. They've stacked their bludgeoning, partisan playbooks on top of their Bibles.

So, how can we keep from slipping into grimy, political bunkers?

// STUDY AND ADMIT

Would you believe someone who said, "I've studied every strain of every political party in the world, and I've come to a completely objective conclusion about which party deserves my loyalty"? Of course not. You'd laugh them out the door. Your politics have been shaped by your family, friends, community, education, and experience. Even the purest attempts at objective reason have been tainted—for better or worse—by our environment.

Your faith background has probably shaped your political leanings more than you know. Before a recent election, I preached a sermon about navigating politics as a Christian. I prepared a seven-minute summary of the book *Five Views on the Church and Politics*,[3] which I kept deleting and then re-adding during my study. The book details five political views, all shaped by different faith traditions. The information enlightens, but I feared it was too academic for a sermon. While in the middle of my sermon, I opted to include it. After the sermon, many people told me how valuable that segment was. It helped them understand both themselves and others better. And more importantly, it forced them to admit that people with wildly different political views also came from Bible-honoring, good-seeking, well-thought-out traditions.

// HONOR BUT DON'T BOW TO THE EMPEROR

First Peter 2:17 shocks me: "Show proper respect to everyone, love the family of believers, fear God, honor the emperor." Most scholars believe Nero was the emperor, although some think the timeline better fits under Domitian's reign. The historian Pliny referred to Domitian as "the beast from hell, sitting in its den and licking blood."[4] He viciously persecuted any who did not proclaim him as Lord and God.

Persecution under Nero is also widely documented: "Therefore, first those were seized who admitted their faith, and then, using the information they provided, a vast multitude were convicted. . . . And perishing they were additionally made into sports: they were killed by dogs by having the hides of beasts attached to them, or they were nailed to crosses or set aflame."[5]

So, no matter which of these two emperors was in power at the time, Peter's original audience understood extreme persecution all too well. In the face of such tyranny, revenge would be the natural human response. But then comes 1 Peter 2:17: "Honor the emperor."

Two thousand years later, Christians still need to hear this command. Name any president in our country's history, and you'll undoubtedly spot a group of "Christians" who disobeyed this verse in regard to him. But how do we obey a verse like this when there are so many variables at play? How do we know when to honor and when to resist (because Christians usually only quote this verse when their choice for president is in office)?

Mark Altrogge gives four helpful keys to clarify what it does and doesn't mean to honor the president:[6]

To honor the President means we recognize that God has placed him there. . . . Romans 13:1-2. No matter how much we disagree with or disapprove of our president, we must realize that God has placed him there to accomplish his own sovereign purpose, as God did with Pharaoh in Moses' day. . . . Since God has placed our president in office [or at least allowed him to be placed], we should speak of him respectfully, not in a dishonoring, mocking way. We should also pray for him and bless him. God commands believers to pray for our leaders and all who are in authority (1 Timothy 2:2). We should bless our president. . . .

To honor the President means we should be subject to him and our government: "Be subject for the Lord's sake to every human institution, whether it be to the emperor as supreme, or to governors as sent by him to punish those who do evil and to praise those who do good. For this is the will of God, that by doing good you should put to silence the ignorance of foolish people" (1 Peter 2:13-14). . . . We may not be happy about taxes or regulations we must follow, but God calls us to obey our government unless it commands us to sin. . . .

To honor our president does not mean we must agree with everything he says or does or that we must commend it or condone it. Or that we cannot speak out for truth and righteousness. To honor our president does not mean that we cannot work within legal means to oppose him and change policies we don't believe are righteous or helpful. To honor our president does not mean we can't express where we feel he is wrong.

To honor our president does not mean that we must obey laws if they require us to disobey God.

Trying to honor the emperor will lead you into gray areas you don't like. If a president ordered you not to pray, well, that's a no-brainer. But what about breaking an ordinance in order to protest a human rights issue, employing an illegal alien whose family is a day away from starvation, or praying "in Jesus' name" at a city council meeting?

The only way to dodge the nuances is to hide in a bunker. So embrace them instead. Welcome to no man's land. Cling to the principles grounding you in truth and love, and offer loads of grace to those whose application of those principles varies from yours.

// TAKE DRASTIC MEASURES

In the greatest sermon ever preached, the Sermon on the Mount, Jesus teaches us to look below the surface of sin. He takes aim at the sin beneath the sin. He's concerned about the sins of the heart, which later surface as more obvious transgressions:

> You have heard that it was said, "You shall not commit
> adultery." But I tell you that anyone who looks at a woman
> lustfully has already committed adultery with her in his heart.
> If your right eye causes you to stumble, gouge it out and throw
> it away. It is better for you to lose one part of your body than
> for your whole body to be thrown into hell.
>
> MATTHEW 5:27-29

When God convicted me about my dual allegiance, I wasn't sure how to repent. I still believed we desperately needed hardworking Christians in government and a vocal church in society. But I had gone far overboard.

After prayer and thought, I concluded that the wisest step for me was to *gouge out* political action from my life, at least for a time. Since I hadn't handled it well initially, I needed to admit my incapacity.

Family and friends probably wondered why I suddenly withdrew from the political scene. I didn't talk about it with many people. I quit consuming it. I was just trying to find my way.

Could you benefit from a similar, radical fast from politics? I hear people say, "I watch the news and I get so mad." So quit watching the news! This world doesn't need you to ingest more partisan opinions.

What we really need is for you to love us. We need you to be at peace in your soul. We need you to be gentle and caring. We need you to notice the hurting and lonely.

Apply Jesus' words. If your right-wing media causes you to sin, gouge it out. It's better for your radio to go to hell than your whole body. And if your left-wing media causes you to sin, toss it out. It's better for your TV to go to hell than your whole body.

Don't be ashamed if you can't navigate politics in a healthy way right now. Just get healthy.

// EXTEND GRACE

I once heard Andy Stanley say to a group of leaders, "Make a difference, not a point. Never sacrifice influence for the sake of making a political point." He wasn't advocating a complete political withdrawal, but he was cautioning leaders from making sharp, alienating barbs that would prevent people from hearing the gospel. I use this filter often. You should too.

Several years ago when the Chicken War erupted over the national debate surrounding gay marriage, a preacher publicly chided fellow preachers who'd remained silent on the feud. He warned that silence equaled a wimpy surrender to political correctness—a watering-down of the gospel. I respect this leader. I share his disdain for any watering-down of the gospel, but can't we grant some grace to those choosing to address political matters differently than we do? Doesn't context matter?

I noticed Stanley had not made a public statement, and then I remembered his quote. I wondered what might've been happening in his life. What if he'd just befriended three cynical, unbelieving guys, who all happened to carry a heavy opinion about that cultural debate? What if they were watching his every move? If Stanley made a sharp public statement, he might've risked the only opportunity he'd ever have to share the gospel with those three hypothetical guys. He would've made a point but sacrificed making a difference. I don't know his situation. And if I don't know his situation, don't you think I should grant him a little bit of grace?

It's time to lay off the abrasive judgment of those who pocket their political preferences. Perhaps they have an opportunity to introduce a soul to the light of life, and if so, it is better not to shred that opportunity on a political hill.

CHURCH STEPS

Dr. Perkins holds a remarkable view of the American Constitution: "[It] is the greatest literary work by mankind, but we've been piecemealing it bit by bit. All along we had the right blueprint, but we've only been giving freedom as we choose."[7] America isn't beyond hope, but we've never been worthy of worship.

I fear the American church has forfeited our prophetic voice in society. We turned partisan agendas into makeshift idols, and the world noticed. The world saw us rip candidates of one party for immoral behavior, only to excuse wretchedness from candidates from our party of choice. They saw us slant facts to win arguments. They saw us attack people—actual human beings. We showed our cards. Political victories mattered more than integrity and love.

Perhaps you contributed nothing to the problem. Thank you. However, much of the world lumps us all together. We share this problem, so much work needs to be done. Is your church committed to it?

Dick Alexander, a respected preacher and consultant, wrote, "I think there are two errors—one is to use the government to enforce a Christian agenda. Evangelical Christians have had 40 bad years in America trying to win 'culture wars.' The other error is to hide in a 'Christian' bubble. The New Testament refers to government in two ways. Revelation calls it Babylon the Great, the great whore. Yet the Apostle Paul calls it a minister of God. Paradoxically it's BOTH. On any given day, a government can be one or the other."[8]

We find ourselves living in tension. When the tension feels too tense, we can ask ourselves, "What is God cheering on? What's at the top of his agenda?" He's rooting for the church to be the church, his Kingdom to flourish, truth to be preached, hearts to be changed, and believers to be united. He's applauding when Christians live such good lives, even in the arena of politics, that unbelievers see Christ through us.

The time I spent with politics removed from my life helped me renew my love and allegiance to the Kingdom. I believe I've healed a lot. If you want to visit about politics, I won't duck underneath the table anymore. I listen to presidential debates and stay informed. I vote, when I can in good conscience. I won't dodge political subjects when a sermon demands them. In all these things, I'll try to proceed with caution, humility, and gentleness. Encourage your church friends to do whatever they must to honor God with their politics. If the church intentionally or unintentionally ostracizes people with diverse political leanings, we've departed from the path of Jesus. But when we stick to the Kingdom playbook, people find truth and peace.

People are gracious and warmed when they hear Christians speak about politics without joining a bunker. This is done so rarely that it catches people off guard. If we can leave the bunkers full of racial and political slipperiness, we deserve to dance. The rest of the bunkers seem manageable, right? So let's keep dancing toward freedom.

REFLECTION QUESTIONS

1. What has shaped your political views?

2. What kind of political stance would someone have to take in order for you to quit caring about their soul? Has your anger over political differences usurped your compassion for that person?

3. Do you think you need to become more informed or less consumed with national politics? What steps should you take to do so?

4. Do you listen to and learn from people with different political perspectives?

5. With the political leader whom you most dislike, do you encourage others to hate him/her, or do you encourage others to pray for him/her? Take time to pray now and commit to praying as you move forward.

CHAPTER 16

CLASS WARFARE

Give me neither poverty nor riches, but give me only my daily bread. Otherwise, I may have too much and disown you and say, "Who is the LORD?" Or I may become poor and steal, and so dishonor the name of my God.

PROVERBS 30:8-9

DRIVE THROUGH ALMOST ANY neighborhood in the world and you can deduce the socioeconomic status of the people who live there. The economically rich live by the rich, go to school with the rich, shop with the rich, and eat with the rich. The poor huddle in South Chicago, East St. Louis, or whatever part of the city becomes *their place.*

A simple glance accuses: *Your poverty defines you; you are lazy and foolish,* or *Your wealth defines you; you are greedy and oppressive.* The lone cousin still at the bottom rung of the financial ladder and the lone friend who climbed out of his neighborhood's poverty both catch condescending glares. Rifts spread from our hearts to our families to our cities.

The more you look at me with contempt (because I have more than you or less than you), the more my contempt of you will grow. Both of us will suffer.

Class warfare is a system of bunkers dug by assumptions, attitudes, and lack of compassion. But what if we could bury the notion of class warfare? What if we could replace socioeconomic bunkers with bridges?

FLANNEL

The way Kelvin's shoulders sank made him appear smaller than he really was—six foot four. Our church's food pantry bustled that night, and the room full of needs and kids made him nervous. "We'll get you squared away with some food in a moment, but I wondered if we could pray for you first," I said after visiting with him about his situation.

Leaning in, as if confessing a sin, Kelvin said in a hushed tone, "I've been wanting to come to your church on a Sunday, but this is all I have to wear. I don't have anything nicer." He tugged on his faded pants and flannel shirt, as if to prove how unacceptable they were.

Matt, my good friend and a new volunteer, was learning the ropes of our ministry that night. He sat with us. Matt's heart is bigger than the welding warehouse where he employs a dozen guys, many thankful someone gave them a second chance. You should know two other things about Matt: He can take a joke, and he dresses quite comfortably on Sundays. He typically dons shorts, flip-flops, hoodies, or Pittsburgh Steelers jerseys (bless his heart).

I winked at Matt and then turned to Kelvin. "I promise you, no matter what you wear, you'll always look sharper than Matt! Really, what you're wearing right now is not only acceptable, it's normal."

He wasn't convinced. "Will I really fit in? Will people really be okay with me wearing this?"

"Yes, Kelvin. Matt really will wear something like what he's wearing right now. I will dress similarly to what I'm wearing now too, and I'm the preacher." Kelvin sat back and nodded.

Have you ever been the most underdressed person at a fancy event, feeling self-conscious like Kelvin? Whether anyone notices or not, it feels as if every eyeball is on you. Maybe this is why the book of James illustrates the sin of favoritism by telling a story about a man dressed in filthy rags. The host orders the poor guest to sit on the floor, while the rich guest receives royal treatment (2:1-9). If you're paying attention, you know the story; you'll see it happen around you every day.

Tulsa's new downtown library has become one of my favorite places to read and write. The free parking, comfortable work spaces, computers, design tools, books, training classes, and coffee shops lure an economically diverse crowd inside. The only thing that costs money is the coffee. I often see a number of homeless folks working on computers or reading magazines. I love everything about it, but my friend doesn't share my views: "There's so many homeless in there. I wish they could make one part of the library just for them, so we could be separated." That's precisely the kind of attitude James strongly warned against: "Have you not discriminated among yourselves and become judges with evil thoughts?" (James 2:4).

We all face this temptation, especially those of us who live relatively privileged lives. It's easy to see our experience as "normal" and those different from us as "less than." But the reality of who we are in Christ should humble us and keep us from that kind of partiality.

The biblical word for *partiality* means "face-taking."[1] When we say that a judge should be impartial, we mean that the judge should not take the face of a person into account when making his or her ruling. (I'd be in big trouble if they did so. I'm told I sometimes have a smirk on my face, and that smirk grows when I'm under the microscope. A face-taking judge would lock me up for a very long time.)

Partiality denies some while giving to others. Even in the early church, we see Christians falling into the trap of partiality.

God worked overtime to motivate Paul, Peter, and the early church to eliminate favoritism. A series of conversions, journeys, miracles, and meetings finally set the record straight: Gentiles can follow Jesus without keeping all of the Jewish regulations. Peter concluded, "I now realize how true it is that God does not show favoritism."[2]

If even God rejects favoritism, whether it be economic or spiritual, so must we. Those with more economic resources must treat the person with less with equality and respect. And those with less must graciously accept the person with more. As followers of Christ, we must fight against the urges to feel superior, inferior, jealous, or arrogant.

BLAME GAME

Jesus' parable of the Good Samaritan tells of a man robbed, beaten, and left for dead on the side of the road. Read the entire parable in Luke 10 to see the surprising hero, but I want to mention one detail: Nobody blames the victim. It wasn't his fault that robbers attacked him. He's not scolded for a lack of planning, caution, or kung fu training. He's just a man in need of help. The villains of the story are the robbers, along with those who later walk by without helping.

When the Bible talks about the poor, it rarely places blame on them. The blame falls on the shoulders of an oppressive king, crooked economic system, or unfair judicial system. And sometimes the plight of the poor is simply the result of a bad harvest or family tragedy.

Those with resources should reject the urge to assign blame to the person in need. If you are quick to blame, you'll be slow to help (at best). Blaming others for their misfortune is an attempt to soothe a guilty conscience. There's a time and place for peeling the layers contributing to poverty, but real help looks differently than judgmental blame.

But in the midst of the poverty we see every day, it can be hard to know what to do. We can't do everything, but we must do something. Confusion can usher in apathy or foolishness. Thankfully the Bible teaches us so much about the subject. The book of Proverbs speaks of four responsibilities—two aimed at the person with extra and two aimed at all of us. If you personally accept these responsibilities, you'll be prepared to avoid the bunkers of class warfare. And churches and charities, you also share these responsibilities. I encourage you to review them with your leaders and teach them to your people.

// 1. I'M RESPONSIBLE FOR HELPING THE POOR.[3]

Don't you hate the awkward moment when you pretend to not see a homeless guy, but you can tell he knows exactly what you're doing? God has some sharp words for those who ignore or refuse the poor:

> Do not exploit the poor because they are poor
>   and do not crush the needy in court,
> for the LORD will take up their case
>   and will exact life for life.

PROVERBS 22:22-23

> Whoever oppresses the poor shows contempt for their Maker,
>   but whoever is kind to the needy honors God.

PROVERBS 14:31

(*also see* PROVERBS 14:21; 19:17; 21:13; 29:7; 31:9; *and then read* MATTHEW 25)

One afternoon in a bookstore café, I brushed by a man in need. He spoke not one word to me. He didn't need to; his face told the story. But I had important things to do. As it turns out, so did God.

When my hand reached for the door, I heard Proverbs 14:31 in my heart. By the time I stepped outside, the Spirit's whisper escalated into a roar. I repented and walked back into the store. I think God was saying, "I'm sorry you forced me to raise my voice." I'm glad he did. I made a friend over a cup of hot chocolate that day.

Giving to those in need is the best antidote to greed I know. The Bible repeatedly warns about the danger of money and what it can do to us.

> Those who want to get rich fall into temptation and a trap
> and into many foolish and harmful desires that plunge people
> into ruin and destruction. For the love of money is a root of
> all kinds of evil. Some people, eager for money, have wandered
> from the faith and pierced themselves with many griefs.

1 TIMOTHY 6:9-10

The love of money ensnares the greedy and oppresses the weak. Both cause widespread destruction. But giving to the person in need can save both.

The Father commanded us to care for his children, Jesus modeled it, and the Holy Spirit keeps reminding us.

Caring for the poor is a matter of justice. Biblical justice says that all people are created in the image of God: the annoying lady next door, the Wall Street businessman, and the trafficked boy on the other side of the globe. All people deserve compassion, regardless of their age, ethnicity, morality, or mistakes.

The person refusing to extend care to the poor lives in a bunker cursed by God (Matthew 25). You'd be hard-pressed to find a position more often rebuked in the Bible. So we must begin by seeking God's compassion for those in need.

// 2. I'M RESPONSIBLE FOR BEING WISE IN HELPING THE POOR.

Proverbs 11:15-17 says, "Whoever puts up security for a stranger will surely suffer, but whoever refuses to shake hands in pledge is safe. A kindhearted woman gains honor, but ruthless men gain only wealth. Those who are kind benefit themselves, but the cruel bring ruin on themselves." Seeking to follow the way of compassion toward the poor does not mean we need to set aside wisdom. In fact, wisdom and compassion must go hand in hand.

One bunker says, "Only the heart matters, so give without looking." Another says, "Only the mind matters, so I don't waste my money on others." Our path forward values both the heart and the mind.

A monumental moment occurred for our church when our food pantry team acknowledged, "It's possible for us to hurt the very people we want to help." Everyone on that team ached for the hungry and needy. But when study and research enlightened us to the dreadful impact of ill-advised benevolence, everything changed. From then on, giving a heartfelt effort wasn't good enough. We carry the responsibility to be good stewards of the resources God has entrusted to us. Effectiveness matters.

James Whitford teaches, "Compassion is the fuel, charity is the vehicle, justice is the destination."[4] How we carry out charity, how we deliver it, makes all the difference in the world. The story of a young man from Rwanda illustrates hurtful charity:

> Jano was vibrant and innovative and recognized there was an opportunity for him to start a business selling eggs in his community. So he bought chickens and began selling eggs. His business was successful and began growing rapidly. Jano also was growing in prominence and sought positive change in his community.
>
> At the same time, a church in Georgia was in the midst of exploring helping the poor globally. They recognized they had a tremendous abundance of resources and wanted to help those in need. . . . They recognized there was a huge protein shortage in the orphanage [which the church visited in Rwanda]. . . . They arranged for hundreds of thousands of eggs to be delivered over a few years and distributed freely in the community they had visited. . . .
>
> What happened as a result of their charity was some short-term relief—but a lot of long-term harm. Jano, the egg seller, was unable to compete with free eggs. He had been growing his business and becoming a leader in his community. As a result of the hundreds of thousands of dollars of free eggs, he had to sell all of his chickens. Along with the rest of the egg sellers who were starting to emerge in this country, he had to close up shop. The market was then flooded with chickens, and he lost a lot of money as a result of the church's newest program.
>
> It sadly gets worse. While there were undoubtedly individuals who were healthier during those three years, when the church's program ended and they decided to re-direct their missions budget funding to a project in South Africa, the community in Rwanda was left out to dry. They now were at

a worse point than when the church began the project as they now had no eggs and nobody in the community to buy them from. Good intentions are not enough.[5]

Foolishly designed charities, like foolishly designed welfare systems, do for the poor what enabling parents do for their kids. They strip people of both dignity and responsibility, leaving them ill-equipped for work and life. It's a lazy cop-out to be in the habit of saying, "Oh well, God will judge them if they misuse it," when we could be saying, "I believe my generosity will help them improve their situation." We can never guarantee anything when trying to help someone, but we can certainly exercise great wisdom before we do.

Foolishly designed charities also harm those trying to help the poor. If volunteers see their charity causing harm or enabling ungratefulness, they'll grow jaded. They'll lose the compassion they once had, and they'll either quit serving with compassion or walk away from the charity altogether.

Unwise charities push the helper and the helped into opposing bunkers. But wise charities restore dignity, responsibility, hope, and relationships. Proverbs unveils a healthy balance: We must engage both our hearts and our minds to help the poor. Churches and charities must hit the books and the streets as they turn their compassion into charity.[6]

I'm so proud of how our church's food pantry has grown in wisdom and effectiveness. The smallest adjustments can make a big difference. When our team started prioritizing clients who took the effort to call and make an appointment, *responsibility* was raised. When we arranged the pantry so clients could peruse the shelves and pick their own food, *dignity* was raised. Small, wise changes made the difference.

// 3. I'M RESPONSIBLE FOR WORKING DILIGENTLY.

Entitlement occurs when someone believes they are owed what someone else produced. Proverbs warns the "entitled," knowing the attitude would harm them and tempt people to join an opposing bunker. There's no excuse to despise the poor. Ever. But that in and of itself is no excuse for anyone to tempt the rich to despise them—and nothing does this quite like laziness. If you'd like to avoid the Bible comparing you to a slug, you'd better work hard:

A sluggard buries his hand in the dish;
  he will not even bring it back to his mouth!
PROVERBS 19:24

Those who work their land will have abundant food,
  but those who chase fantasies have no sense.
PROVERBS 12:11[7]

People often chase fantasies instead of wisdom and hard work. Casinos are designed to make people feel like movie stars. Commercials imply that buying a product will enhance your image. Dreams and goals require hard work, but fantasies are for the sluggards.

God expects people to work hard. Even before the curse in the Garden of Eden, Adam worked. Although the curse has soiled our work experience, work itself is not part of the curse. We were created to work. The biblical ideal is for people to work, taking care of themselves, their families, their church, and the stranger as well. When people can't work, they need not feel shame, but instead thank the Lord for how he provides, while graciously offering of themselves what they can (prayers, encouragement, service, etc.).

Last week, a woman visited our food pantry. She worked hard and had almost enough to survive another month but needed a few additional items to feed her family. We were glad to help her, but before we could, she said she had something for us. She'd heard about an organization giving away extra peanut butter, so she took the time to get some. They gave her way more peanut butter than she needed, so she wanted to donate it to us, so we could give it to others. Hearing about her effort to get the peanut butter and her generosity to give it away lifted our spirits. She reminded us that we are all on the same team, working together. She made it easy to be generous with her. The path to freedom is lined with disciplined work, sharing, and thoughtfulness.

// 4. I'M RESPONSIBLE FOR GIVING CREDIT TO GOD.

Sometimes ivory towers can fit in a bunker. In the towers are people who believe all their success, money, and possessions are only a result of their savvy minds or hard work. They share no credit with God or anyone else. Pride consumes them.

Success will destroy us if we believe the age-old lie "I earned it on my own; I deserve it." Proverbs 30:8-9 identifies this concern: "Give me neither poverty nor riches, but give me only my daily bread. Otherwise, I may have too much and disown you and say, 'Who is the LORD?' Or I may become poor and steal, and so dishonor the name of my God."

All gifts come from God. The ability to work, think, and study comes from him. We give thanks for every penny and piece of bread. And a gracious spirit flows from our thankfulness and contentment.

When we commit to all four of these principles, we are able to look upon our lives with confidence and joy, just as Paul did.

> I have not coveted anyone's silver or gold or clothing. You
> yourselves know that these hands of mine have supplied my
> own needs and the needs of my companions. In everything I
> did, I showed you that by this kind of hard work we must help
> the weak, remembering the words the Lord Jesus himself said:
> "It is more blessed to give than to receive."
>
> ACTS 20:33-35

BLESSED

The Bible tells the story of Jesus giving up his riches and becoming poor so we might be rich—spiritually rich, filled and whole.[8] Every human on the planet faces spiritual poverty. We stand on even ground, helpless but not hopeless. A proper perspective lets the millionaire and the homeless man view each other as equals. Only God warrants praise. The rest of us need him, and we need each other.

I saw an extraordinary illustration of this kind of Christ-infused response in India. Beth and I had the joy to visit and work with good friends in this beautiful land for a week in 2016. The people of India are kind and extreme in their generosity (and their exquisite cooking added five pounds to my waistline).

A dark aspect that remains in India, however, is the caste system, which divides people into different social levels based solely on birth. I'd read about the caste system, but experiencing it was something I won't forget. I won't pretend to know its complexity, how it varies in different regions, or when it blurs with hospitality, but I learned a little bit. My good friend Vivert explained, "If someone is born the son of a barber, they will be a barber. If their parent farms, so too will they. Our society allows for nothing else, although some of our Christians [about 2 percent of the population] view this differently."

Later that week, I was to teach a group of church planters. Many of these men suffered greatly for their commitment to Christ and ministry. They'd been ostracized from families, friends, and home villages. Some had survived vicious persecution from extremists. One showed me the scar from where a sword hit his head when their church was attacked. One of his members lost her unborn baby that day. Yet these men pressed on, and the gospel was spreading like wildfire. People full of despair responded in droves to the love and hope of God. I'd never felt less worthy to speak to an audience.

A joyful buzz of conversation echoed down the hallway as I walked toward the lecture hall. I couldn't understand a word of it, but I could tell these guys were more than casual friends. Nothing tightens the bonds of friendship more than suffering. I failed at stepping unnoticed into the back of the room. Cluster by cluster, they saw me, quieted, and stood in respect. Eighty giants gave reverent attention to someone unworthy to tie their shoes.

My time with those men, both during our sessions and in private conversations later, blessed me beyond measure. I'll not forget. Through their shared faith in Christ, these men were able to battle against a societal value system built to show favorites. These men instead showed the Kingdom way, giving love, grace, and hope even in the midst of persecution.

There's no place for socioeconomic bunkers, especially in the church. I'm so thankful for my Indian friends with the courage to speak the love and acceptance of Christ in a culture that tells you where you can or can't sit on the social ladder. The socioeconomic divides in India have their own flair, but they are neither new nor isolated. The gap between poverty and wealth impacts us all.

In their book *Small Matters: How Churches and Parents Can Raise Up World-Changing Children*,[9] Greg Nettle and Santiago "Jimmy" Mellado make the powerful claim that many children suffer from having too little, and many suffer from having too much. The casualties of poverty are easy to see. The casualties of affluence take longer to unfold, yet they are real, indeed. The boy who thinks the world revolves around him becomes the man who thinks the world revolves around him. And he lives empty—empty of perspective, of dependence upon God and others, of thankfulness, and of wisdom. And he probably acts like a spoiled brat.

When people all work hard, care for others, and rely on the Provider, peace reigns. The quickest way to bring people from diverse socioeconomic backgrounds together is to help them start fighting the same battles. What if the rich and poor fought poverty together? What if homeowners and homeless fought housing issues together? What if the fed and the starved fought hunger together? What if we exited our socioeconomic bunkers and brought others with us? Don't you want to belong to a church like that? Don't you want to live in a world like that? Don't you want to walk this path?

Kelvin, the guest in our food pantry, worked up the courage to come to church. The love he received matched the love he gave. A month after his first visit, he shared a Christmas meal with a family from church. They'll tell you how blessed they were.

REFLECTION QUESTIONS

1. How are the socioeconomic classes divided in your city? How are they brought together?

2. Are you more apt to look with disdain at the rich or poor?

3. Has your attempt to help someone ever caused more harm than good?

4. Which of the four responsibilities do you need to accept? How can you do so?

5. Are there some leaders from a church or benevolent ministry with whom you can share this chapter? Pray for your church's efforts to bless those with too little and to provide opportunities for those with plenty.

CHAPTER 17

GENERATIONAL DISCORD

When an old man dies, a library burns to the ground.
AFRICAN PROVERB

ABOUT EVERY TWENTY YEARS, a new generation is born. The babies don't know they are destined to be labeled and stereotyped by "experts." They aren't even aware that the previous generations will gripe about "kids these days!" But it will happen. It always does.

Every new generation disheartens the older generations. If you think this is a recent phenomenon, picture the reaction of two parents whose daughter just divulged she was going to Woodstock. They probably weren't thrilled, right?

While generational discord isn't new, it feels as if the needle has moved toward volatility. I see it on both ends of the spectrum. Hardly a week goes by without another article demeaning Millennials (born between 1980 and 2000). I've wondered if there's a clandestine contest to see who can say the most disparaging things about Millennials. The thing about generalizations is that even if they are played for laughs, they can be hurtful and unhelpful.

But on the other end of the spectrum, our entire culture has torched respect for the elderly. Many places on this planet have not made this same mistake, but America's addiction to power, money, beauty, and athleticism corrupts us. We take for granted and even look down on the wisdom and perspective of our elders.

The more one age group demeans, belittles, or ignores the other, the more both press further into their bunkers. Those bunkers have gotten really deep, even though I rarely hear this labeled as a major concern.

Learning how to honor and respect people no matter their generation is vital if we're going to move forward into freedom.

KNOCKING DOWN LEAVES

Lots of lonely people live in our church's neighborhood. Some of them have just purchased their first house. They're launching into adult life, working their first real jobs, and looking for friendships. They may have a crying baby and no family support. They'd do anything for an older couple to adopt them.

Others have lived in the neighborhood for forty years. Their spouses have passed away, friends have moved away, things have changed, and they feel isolated and scared.

Every year our church sends flyers to our neighbors. We offer to rake leaves, clean gutters, and mow lawns on an upcoming Sunday. We've served people with sicknesses, family crises, and disabilities. Some of the projects have required hours of manpower. But sometimes we're asked to help someone with a nicely groomed yard. They may only ask us to pick up a few sticks or leaves. At first this bothered me, because I thought they wasted our time. That was before I met Mary.

Mary asked us to change one outside light bulb and paint one post. She had all the needed supplies set out neatly on a table, and she immediately served hot chocolate to everyone in the group. Both projects took a combined twenty minutes of labor. Since there wasn't much for most of us to do, we sat on her porch and visited. She told us about her terminal cancer. She told us about her sick daughter. She talked and talked. We listened, hugged, and prayed.

Mary didn't need any yard work done. She needed friends. Ever since that day, we tell our teams not to rush. Their best ministry may be visiting on the porch. We suspect every year a few elderly widows use a broom to knock down some leaves from their trees. It's just an excuse— an excuse to be loved.

This goes for people of any age in our communities. No matter the generation, we long for love, friendship, and acceptance. If you grew up in a close-knit family, consider the feeling you had at Thanksgiving dinner. Holiday meals are a special, joyful time for healthy families. Everyone works together. Grandpa keeps everyone entertained with funny or important family stories. Grandma whispers a word of encouragement as she passes by a quiet child. The aunts and uncles work hard preparing the food in the kitchen. The teenagers tell Grandpa to rest his back while they fetch the extra chairs. The cousins talk about life as they wash the dishes. No one is more important than anyone else. Everyone matters.

When families, churches, and communities capture this spirit, we find ourselves on the same path. When everyone matters more than our bunkers, it's suddenly easier to leave those bunkers.

BUILDING INTERGENERATIONAL UNITY

Jack Foreman is one of my favorite people in the world. He's refused to allow the status of "widower" to prevent him from living a full and meaningful life. He spends his time volunteering to help the hungry, caring for friends, gathering eggs from his chickens, chopping wood (even when the doctors advise it's not a good idea after shoulder surgery), playing piano, and baking bread or pies to give away (did I mention he's a bit of a Renaissance man?). Jack has a way of connecting with the young and the old alike. As I've watched him, I've learned godly ways we, too, can build intergenerational unity.

// 1. GIVE

In 1 Timothy 5, Paul gave age-specific instructions for the church. You could sum up the instructions with one word: *give*. This principle still serves us well. Young men, give your respect and your strong backs to the older men. Older men, give your time and wisdom to the younger men. Young women, give your encouragement and help to the older women. Older women, give your knowledge and compassion to the younger women. Children, give your honor to your parents. Parents, give your love to your children. Give, give, give.

Over the past few years, Jack has hosted several of our church interns. We joke that his house is not just temporary housing, it's a bed-and-breakfast. An awesome young guy named Zach served as preaching intern for us one year. (We don't require interns have names that rhyme with Jack, but it certainly helps). When he came into my office the first morning, I said, "How was the smoothie?" He smiled and replied, "Oh, Jack always makes breakfast for his guests?" Then he added, "He offered to do my laundry, too. I declined at first, but he told me he really enjoys doing laundry, so I finally agreed. Now I feel kinda bad." I laughed and advised, "You may as well submit to Jack's kindness. He's a giver."

Giving crushes the spirit of entitlement. Giving breaks down walls. Giving prompts others to give. Giving puts us on the path to freedom.

// 2. RECEIVE

Our culture preaches independence to a dangerous extreme. We often won't accept help, and we definitely won't ask for it. It's caused isolation, and bunkers are built on isolation.

Paul wrote that it's more blessed to give than to receive, which is true, but for most people, it's more difficult to receive than to give. Our pride, and sometimes just our concern for others, gets in the way of receiving help.

On the first Sunday of every month, our church asks everyone to consider giving an extra dollar. Then, we count everyone there and set aside one dollar per attendee. If 275 people are counted, we allot $275 to our Dollar Difference Team, who are always scouring the church family for needs. When a tornado destroyed the auto shop and some personal tools of a young newlywed guy in the church, the Dollar Difference Team asked him if he'd be willing to receive that month's gift. He agreed, and as he accepted a gift card to a hardware store, tears streamed down his face.

I had the joy of telling our church about the recipient of that gift. As I told the story, I noticed an elderly couple grinning from ear to ear. They were overjoyed to help this young man. They were blessed to give. He blessed them by receiving.

Zach did a good thing by allowing Jack to do his laundry. Jack loves to help people, especially young people, so in a crazy way, Zach blessed Jack by allowing him to give. Later that summer, Zach was glad to help Jack with some yard projects. Zach was blessed that Jack received. Do you see how this works?

Older friends, ask for and receive the help given by the younger. As they serve you, they will love you more and more. Younger friends, ask for and receive help from the older. You'll learn, you'll laugh, and as they pour their lives into you, they will love you more and more.

Willingness to receive allows others to give, find purpose, and experience joy. It also allows the receiver to learn humility, dependence, and thankfulness. It's a beautiful gift on the path to freedom.

// 3. FIND AND BE A MENTOR

Do not rebuke an older man harshly, but exhort him as if he were your father. Treat younger men as brothers, older women as mothers, and younger women as sisters, with absolute purity.

I TIMOTHY 5:1-2

Paul exhorted Timothy to help the church act as a loving family. Paul not only instructed with words but also modeled it with his life. He'd taken Timothy, a much younger man, under his wing and mentored him to be a church leader. Together, Paul and Timothy lived out generational unity.

My life has been shaped by people who intentionally mentored me. They built a relationship with me, listened to me, and imparted wisdom to me. They cared enough to hold me accountable and to demand my best. One such mentor, over a period of two decades, invested in the lives of dozens of young men in college. I will never forget the evening we surprised him with a thank-you party. He said with confidence, "I've written many books and spoken to crowds of thousands, but you are my greatest legacy."

Who will be your legacy?

My friend Halee received motherly care from a godly, powerhouse woman from our church. Halee wrote,

Being very pregnant, I awoke early one morning knowing something wasn't right with the baby. My husband was unable to go with me to the hospital. So, at 6:30 a.m., I called my friend Pam.

"Hello," Pam said.

"I'm so sorry to call you this early. I didn't want to wake you," I said, feeling guilty.

"Actually, sweetheart—I think I was waiting for you to call."

She had apparently also woken early with a strong leading to read James 1—a chapter filled with insights of withstanding hardships. The Lord had prepared Pam for this moment.

At the hospital, she looked at the same ultrasound as I did, showing the lifeless body of our son, Elliot. Pam called my husband, and she remained with us until we held our son in our arms at 11 p.m. that night.

This was not the first nor the last time Pam invested in me. God used her to play a vital role in my learning to forgive a past abuser, which was a turning point in my life. She and her husband mentored my husband and me during our engagement and marriage. She was in the room when our oldest son was born, and we've grown together in ministry.

Pam has not always been perfect in her role—she is just a woman with physical and emotional limits—which means that I cannot fully rely on her to meet my needs. Her contagious love for the Lord points me back to my one true Healer, Jesus Christ.

Every time I see Pam and her husband, I hope they notice my heart leaping with joy. I am committed to love her back and to pass the baton to others whom God puts in my life.

Investing in younger people, and being invested in by older people, is an incredible blessing. Have you asked God to place some people in your life who need someone, imperfect but willing, to mentor them? Have you asked for someone to mentor you? Can you start by asking someone to lunch, asking, "What did you learn as a father?" or "I know your job has changed—how are you doing?" or "How did you balance work and family?" Be intentional to build relationships with those older and younger than you. You may be amazed by what God does.

CHURCH STEPS

The illustration of the healthy family at a holiday meal, each serving the other, is the kind of interaction I love to see within a church context. I cast this vision often, because a healthy church emulates a healthy family. Young serve the old and old serve the young. As leaders, we don't seek to appease either group. Trying to appease everyone is a losing game. Businesses try to appease customers. Churches don't want customers. We want family. We talk about acknowledging all people who come, and we try to find ways to love them.

Healthy intergenerational relationships are important in our lives as individuals, and they are vital in the body of Christ. What can your church do to promote generational unity?

Value it. Who is the best person to give advice to a young mom? Who has the time and desire to help a young family care for a baby? Who does an elderly man with a bad back need to help him move the couch? This isn't rocket science here. We need *each other*, so we should begin by valuing other generations.

Get intentional about it. We gravitate toward those who are like us. Left to our own instincts, we'll surround ourselves with people our age. This means the church will need to intentionally counteract this. Churches can value multigenerational ministries, staffs, and small groups.

A young adult recently told me he was bummed to learn that his new small group would be multigenerational. He assumed the mixed group would not be as vulnerable and open with each other. Six weeks later he'd reversed his thoughts. He told me the best surprise of his small group was how well the diverse generations connected and complemented each other.

As for the generational bickering, complaining, and fighting, knock it off. It's stupid, short-sighted, and sinful. It's time to quit fighting for our bunkers and start fighting for each other. If Christians would be obedient to Philippians 2:3—"Do nothing out of selfish ambition or vain conceit. Rather, in humility value others above yourselves"—the old guard would be fighting for the younger people, the younger people would be speaking on behalf of those older, and we'd all be better for it.

Dream about it. One hour of praying and dreaming about how you could promote multigenerational unity could change your life and your church's trajectory. I bet you'd be surprised at the ideas the young and old could dream by talking and listening to each other.

REFLECTION QUESTIONS

1. Has your family and environment shown you a healthy picture of generational unity? How?

2. Who has mentored/invested in you? What did this look like?

3. Are you investing in someone younger than you? Whom? If not, is there someone on your radar?

4. What are some ways your church could promote generational unity?

5. Would you schedule one hour of praying and dreaming about how you (or your family, friends, or church) could promote multigenerational unity?

CHAPTER 18

FAITH FIGHTS

———

Whatever disunites man from God, also disunites man from man.
EDMUND BURKE

I HESITATE TO MENTION THIS to those of you who missed it, because ignorance is bliss, but I'll divulge that in the 1990s, more than a few churches were fighting "worship wars." I wish I were talking about some sort of "battle of the bands," but these wars were bitter disputes about the style of music people used to worship God. I'm serious. Christians argued, bickered, lobbied, and even split churches over a style of music. Some wanted faster songs, others slower, some wanted traditional, others contemporary. People defined their own terms (*traditional* could mean 1970s or 1570s, and *contemporary* could mean 1970s or only the current year).

Sadly, this wasn't the church's last or first fight.

Isaac Watts was one of the greatest hymn writers of all time. He penned songs such as "Joy to the World" and "When I Survey the Wondrous Cross" in the early 1700s. Even then, church folks began arguing about whether it was okay to sing those newfangled, man-made hymns along with their singing of the Psalms. Some churches reached a compromise—they'd sing Psalms before the sermon and hymns after it. However, as a sign of protest against the hymns, some members marched out of the church building after the sermon. Watts retaliated with the hymn "We're Marching to Zion." The second stanza says, "Let those refuse to sing / Who never knew our God; / But children of the heav'nly King . . . / May speak their joys abroad." Wow. Nothing like using a hymn to zing your adversaries.[1]

Similar shameful battles have been waged in the church for a long time. It was an embarrassment then, and it's an embarrassment now. Lights that should've been shining from a hill were buried under petty squabbles.

If two soldiers in the same unit are fighting each other, they may kill each other, they will cause harm to their fellow soldiers nearby, and they won't even notice the approaching enemy.

When Christians fight about a style of music, a budget decision, a denominational squabble, or a method of ministry, the church loses. Our faith should be the last place we find bunkers, but it turns out, we're just as prone to them in the place where our unity should be the greatest.

CAGED BIBLES

Scot McKnight writes about once seeing a strange visitor, a parakeet, in his backyard.[2] It dived, dipped, looped, and flew all around, which was only surprising for one reason: He'd never seen a parakeet free from a cage. Now that I think about it, neither have I.

McKnight began thinking about how we attempt to do with Scripture as we do with a parakeet—we cage it. We attempt to lock God's Word within the bars of our doctrine, tradition, background, or preference. Strict Calvinists (those who adhere to the teachings of the sixteenth-century theologian John Calvin) follow Calvin's teachings, down to the very last letter. (By the way, I have some friends who do this, and they are my brothers and sisters in Christ; I chose this illustration not to jab them—for they could correctly jab back—but because it serves its purpose well.) Calvinist theology is most known for the acronym TULIP.

Each letter stands for a core tenet of Calvinism. The *I* stands for *irresistible grace*. That means that if God gives grace to you, there is nothing in the world that you can do to resist it and thwart God's intention to take you to heaven. Is there truth to the teaching that God's grace is more desirable than anything in the world? Yes. Is there truth to the teaching that God initiates contact with us first, inviting us into his grace? Yes. Can the teaching of irresistible grace become a cage? Yes.

The Bible teaches not only how wonderful God's grace is but also that God has given humankind the opportunity to accept or reject his grace. When Jesus called the rich young ruler to quit worshiping money and to start following him, God's grace got rejected by the man (Mark 10:17-31). He *resisted* God's grace, directly, clearly, unequivocally.

So what do you do with a Scripture like this? It's tempting to try to shove it into a cage and make it say what we want it to say. But does the story of the rich young ruler diminish God's goodness? No. Does it mean humankind holds salvation in their own hands? No. It just means the Bible wasn't meant to be caged into a neat, human-made theological system—not by Calvinists, not by Arminians (an opposing camp to Calvinists), and not by anyone in between. If we submit to God, we allow him and his Word to freely fly, even when it gets uncomfortably distant from our cage. God beckons you to follow his truth, his leading.

Some people reject the idea of any biblical nuance or tension. Their conviction rests in their own cage. This explains how two people can read the same verse from the same Bible and end up in a hotly contested argument. The argument turns into a split. The split turns into two divided groups of believers. And both will be tempted to dig—not into Scripture but into bunkers.

We know this breaks the heart of God, because we can read some of Jesus' last wishes.

LAST WISHES

About one-fourth of John's Gospel is devoted to Jesus' Last Supper. Jesus and his disciples shared this meal on a Thursday night. The Cross came on Friday. Don't miss the intensity of the moments Jesus spent with the men he'd mentored for three years.

Jesus asked two things of his close friends: to remain in his love and to love each other.[3] We shouldn't be surprised by his focus. When Jesus was asked earlier what the greatest commandment was, he replied, "'Love the Lord your God with all your heart and with all your soul and with all your mind.' This is the first and greatest commandment. And the second is like it: 'Love your neighbor as yourself.' All the Law and the Prophets hang on these two commandments" (Matthew 22:37-40).

After having already washed their feet, Jesus repeated the command: "Love each other." The Bible emphasizes this command from cover to cover. This much is plainly obvious: If you aren't loving other people, even the difficult-to-love ones, you aren't following Jesus. To follow Jesus is to let love replace hate.

As the hour of his death drew nearer, Jesus prayed for himself, for his disciples, and for future believers—and that includes us![4] Do you know what Jesus prayed for you? He prayed for something of profound, eternal importance within the body of Christ: unity. Jesus prayed against the lure of bunkers.

Without unity, the world will see a dysfunctional family when it looks at the church. Who wants to join a feuding bunch? But when the world sees unity—even dancing—smack-dab in the middle of a battlefield, our love shines bright. People will wonder how Christians love each other so much. People will be attracted to the diversity. The church will be able to focus on teaching and loving, as opposed to spending their energy putting out relational fires. Above all, God will be glorified, as the perfect unity between the Father, Son, and Holy Spirit glows in God's people.

THE SURPRISING INGREDIENT OF DOCTRINAL ONENESS

Watch your life and doctrine closely.

1 TIMOTHY 4:16

Christians need to hit the pause button before calling a boycott, writing an angry online blurb, or labeling someone a heretic—but they must also reject passivity, trying to wish away the problem. What you believe matters. What your church believes matters. Unity is not the same as pretending disagreements don't exist, and when it comes to disagreements about doctrine and truth, we must be particularly careful. When significant doctrinal rifts enlarge, your church needs to act with precision. You can't afford to botch this one.

Doctrinal oneness requires a surprise ingredient: grace! Not every matter warrants a confrontation. Paul ordered the church in Rome to cease their fighting about dietary regulations.[5] The matter was in no way a test of salvation. Paul labeled it a "disputable matter." We should admit we won't agree about every verse in the Bible, and that's okay.

The Restoration Movement began in the early 1800s with the desire to turn the church away from denominational schisms and toward the faith and unity of the original church in Acts. The movement highlighted the necessity for Christians to discern between what was a matter of absolute doctrine and what was a matter of opinion or preference. Opinions, like private fences (or disputable matters), should be kept in one's backyard. I don't have to give up my private fence (or opinions), but I have no right to force them on others.

"Raccoon" John Smith, who played a pivotal role in the movement, compelled Christians to leave behind needless allegiances and to simply commit to the Bible. Preaching to churches aligned to different leaders (Campbell and Stone), he said, "Let us, then my brethren, be no longer Campbellites or Stoneites, New Lights or Old Lights, or any other kind of lights, but let us come to the Bible, and to the Bible alone, as the only book in the world that can give us all the light we need."[6]

Francis Chan tells the story of a seminary professor who taught, "If you're 51 percent sure of what the Bible says about something, preach it like you are 100 percent."[7] Chan rejected this teaching, understanding that preachers had no right to say things more firmly than God did.

A disgruntled guy once wrote me a nasty letter about my preaching. One of his many problems with me was that he believed a real preacher of God would never say, "I think . . ." or "It's my opinion that . . ." He wanted me to speak only in absolutes. I choose to side with Paul and

Chan on this one. It's a grave error to force personal opinions over the biblical text.

Watching your doctrine closely includes *not making a big deal about stuff that's not a big deal*. A rallying cry for many Christians has been "In essentials, unity; in nonessentials, liberty; and in all things, charity." We still must discern what is an essential, such as *Jesus died for our sins*, and what is a nonessential, such as *How many times should we take Communion in a month?*, but this at least gets us asking the right questions, in love.

If your church watches its doctrine closely, submitting to the God-breathed truths of Scripture while demonstrating discernment and grace in disputable matters, it will live as a healthy body, serving Christ, the head.

REDEFINE *GREATNESS*

The quest for unity gains momentum when the church redefines *greatness* as Christ did. He said, "The greatest among you will be your servant" (Matthew 23:11). This is a tall order, because our world says something else. Greatness, we're told, is measured by power.

Terrell Owens was one of the most dynamic receivers to ever play in the NFL. He ranks third all-time in regular-season receiving touchdowns, and he's second only to Jerry Rice in regular-season receiving yards. Statistics like this make a player a lock to be selected into the Hall of Fame. In 2017, he became eligible. The Hall of Fame declined.

Owens garnered a reputation for causing headaches for coaches, disrupting the unity in locker rooms, and inciting drama within the organization. As his reputation grew, teams hesitated to commit to him, which fueled his angst. Near the end of his career, he jumped from team to team, begging for one more lucrative payday. His career ended when, after he begged teams to give him one more chance, everyone said no.

Owens may still be accepted into the Hall of Fame. For now, he stands rejected. Fair or unfair, the NFL concluded that Owens's negative baggage negated his great talent. There's a lesson for the church here: *Any talent unbowed before the feet of Christ is talent wasted. Resist the urge to be served, and instead, serve. By doing so, you'll build up the church, you'll bring people together, and you'll be found useful in God's Kingdom.*

The entire life of Jesus shouts this upside-down principle:

- *The greatest* is the guy who takes care of orphans.
- *The greatest* is the one who volunteers for the dirtiest job.
- *The greatest* is the lowest.
- *The greatest* gives away power, money, and position.

While in the middle of searching for a new staff member, I heard an axiom from Randy Gariss that guided us well: "Choose people who are better in the back of the room than they are at the front of the room."[8] In other words, seek first humility, integrity, and love. Choose leaders who are capable of leading at the front of the room, of course, but give priority to how they serve others when they are out of the spotlight.

When your church adopts Jesus' definition of greatness, it will fill its leadership teams with servants. Where servants lead and leaders serve, humility permeates the entire congregation. Where humility, integrity, and love are held high, oneness will be the norm.

DISCIPLESHIP: GOD'S PLAN FOR CHURCH UNITY

Apollos was an eloquent, passionate, brilliant orator.[9] He quickly became a force for the early church in Ephesus. Not even the most cunning of Jewish leaders could go toe-to-toe with him in a debate about the claims of Jesus. He crushed the cynics' twisting of Scriptures and denials of Christ. However, Apollos had one glaring flaw: He did not yet understand the baptism of Jesus.

After Jesus had ascended and the disciples were preaching their first post-Resurrection sermon, the listeners asked, "What must we do to be saved?" That's the question every preacher wants to hear! Peter gave the invitation, "Repent and be baptized, every one of you, in the name of

Jesus Christ for the forgiveness of your sins. And you will receive the gift of the Holy Spirit" (Acts 2:38). Three thousand people accepted the invitation, and the church, dripping wet and all, was birthed that very day. From that point on, we see the disciples baptizing those who wanted to follow Jesus, but Apollos had yet to either hear or understand all of this.[10]

Enter Priscilla and Aquila. Dear friends of Paul and faithful servants of Christ, they became aware of both the strengths and the error of Apollos. They could've shamed him publicly, announcing to the church that Apollos was a heretic. They could've publicly argued with him. They could've shunned him. Or they could've ignored his flaw, quietly distancing their ministry from his. Any of these options would've resulted in a division. Perhaps Ephesus would've ended up with two warring churches. Or perhaps Apollos would've walked away from ministry, head drooped in dejection.

But instead of looking to win an argument, Priscilla and Aquila saw an opportunity to disciple and encourage a brother. Instead of dishing out insults, they dished out dessert. They invited him to their home and "explained to him the way of God more adequately" (Acts 18:26).

The opposite of divisiveness in the church is not silence; it's discipleship. There are times when you will be the one who needs to be encouraged and mentored by another, and there will be times when you need to do the building up. Priscilla and Aquila show us how discipleship restores and protects unity.

// 1. DISCIPLESHIP IS RELATIONAL.

Books and online sermons can disciple you some—but only some. Books don't give hugs. Online sermons don't pull you aside to ask how you're applying the lesson. The Bible, church history, and personal experience teach us that effective discipleship comes wrapped in relationships.

You know what this means, right? You have to embrace inconvenience. People are so inconvenient (I'm exhibit A if you'd like to make a case that people are bothersome). We all come loaded with baggage, misconceptions, and oddities.

I once asked a friend far ahead of me in life experience and faith to challenge, encourage, and mentor me. He agreed on one condition: I was never allowed to wonder if I was inconveniencing him. Ever. He knew I'd hesitate to call for help, not because he has ever turned me down, but because we project our own selfish thoughts on others. Relationships require a trust that the other person wants to be with you.

Are you willing to embrace inconvenience in order to build relationships? Discipling someone means you get to know them and love them. And while you learn about their culture, generational values, or financial struggles, the commitment to follow Jesus will build bridges over these differences.

// 2. DISCIPLESHIP IS INSTRUCTIONAL.

I imagine once the dinner was complete, Priscilla and Aquila said, "Our brother, can we talk about doctrine for a bit? We have great news you need to know and teach." Then they instructed him.

Apollos was a brilliant guy, so Priscilla and Aquila had to be well-learned and capable of dancing with theological heavyweights. Maybe you feel like a lightweight. Truth be told, we all should feel that way, so don't fret. God comes to you in grace and then prompts you to move forward. What can you do today to grow in your ability to instruct someone else in the way of the Lord?

Academics, including theological ones, often earn the reputation of being elitists, impersonal and condescending. Academics build lots of bunkers this way. But Priscilla and Aquila nurtured the relational component, even when diving into the instructional. We all learn best when we know the instructor cares for us. How we teach matters.

// 3. DISCIPLESHIP IS INTENTIONAL.

When our kids trail behind at a store, my wife will say, "Walk with a purpose." She wants to cross off the grocery-list items and get on with her day. Priscilla and Aquila discipled with a purpose. They listened intently, invited, instructed, and wrote a letter to prepare the church in Achaia for the arrival of Apollos. Discipleship doesn't happen by accident. Fights do. How often I've heard, "I'm not even sure how the argument first started." Rifts are easy, so set your eyes on unity.

The last verses of Acts 18 say Apollos was a great help to the believers and "vigorously refuted his Jewish opponents in public debate, proving from the Scriptures that Jesus was the Messiah" (verse 28).

Let your faith walk hand in hand with your pursuit of unity. Reject divisive faith talk. Bear with one another. Caring about your church is one thing. Caring for your church is something altogether different.

Paul begged the church, "*Make every effort* to keep the unity of the Spirit through the bond of peace. There is *one* body and one Spirit, just as you were called to *one* hope when you were called; *one* Lord, *one* faith, *one* baptism; *one* God and Father of all, who is over all and through all and in all" (Ephesians 4:3-6, emphasis mine). I believe this is one of the most important passages in the entire Bible. Oh, to be one!

Half-baked efforts won't cut it. Practically, they'll fail. Unity requires every effort. God requires every effort. Are you making every single, sweat-drenched, last-ditch, heart-wrenching, life-giving effort to keep the unity, the oneness? It's time to ask for a commitment, so I'm asking. Right now. Are you on board?

Finally, all of you, be like-minded, be sympathetic, love one another, be compassionate and humble.

I PETER 3:8

How good and pleasant it is
    when God's people live together in unity!

PSALM 133:1

REFLECTION QUESTIONS

1. Have issues of faith caused division in your life? Your church?

2. Why was Jesus so concerned about the church's unity?

3. What "disputable matters" (issues that should be left for opinion) are being mistaken for matters of doctrinal faith (not to be compromised)?

4. How are you intentionally discipling others? Is inconvenience preventing you from discipling someone else?

5. What can you do today to grow in your ability to instruct someone else in the way of the Lord? How can you take a baby step? Pray about this.

EPILOGUE

A Hill on Which to Die

Make every effort to keep the unity of the Spirit through the bond of peace.

EPHESIANS 4:3

IF YOU PLAN TO TAKE ON the work of reconciliation—and I pray you will—you will suffer. Frederick Douglass wrote, "If there is no struggle, there is no progress."[1] You can't push against comforts, systems, and structures without resistance. But when you suffer, take heart in knowing that Jesus understands.

Révérien Rurangwa witnessed the slaughter of his own family during the genocide in Rwanda. He lived but was maimed, becoming a physically marred, emotionally brutalized, homeless refugee. In the midst of his despair, one sudden discovery from his Bible gave him hope: "This Christ, disfigured, bruised, hacked away, pierced, cut, looks like me. . . . He looks like a young Tutsi from the Mugina hillside, dismembered on April 20, 1994, by men who should have been his brothers. He looks like the victim of the Tutsi genocide. He looks like all victims of all genocides, of all massacres, of all crimes, of all wrongs."[2] The gospel provides the framework for healing, justice, and even the unthinkable: forgiveness.

Dr. John Perkins spoke of the inspiration he received by reading about the suffering of the prophets. Faithfulness in dark times spreads light for eternity. Jesus embodied this on the cross. His suffering blankets victims with encouragement in their present and hope for their future.

Suffering, in fact, is part of the answer we give and live as we step out of the bunkers and into no man's land. Job, whose journey through suffering spans forty-two chapters in your Bible, had several friends come to his side. They were wonderful encouragers . . . right until they started talking. Their first response was perfect. They sat and mourned with Job. They entered into his suffering. When we suffer with the wounded, without any personal agenda, hearts will be softened and bridges will be built.

Those in the bunkers suffer without joy, fulfillment, or ultimate hope. As we step into no man's land, we will suffer with a purpose, because Jesus suffered for us. We will suffer with hope, because one day Christ will remove our pain. But we will suffer, nonetheless.

And so, our decision to step into no man's land is not to be taken lightly. We may be ridiculed. We may lose friends and find ourselves standing alone for a time. We must consider our steps very seriously. On what hill are we willing to die? For what are we willing to suffer?

STANDING ON MOUNTAINS

Lots of folks have confused molehills with mountains. They voraciously defend six-inch piles of dirt, the less important things: personal preferences, church traditions, partisan policies. Molehills are no place to take a stand. But Scripture points us toward where we can find our hills to die on:

- *Do not be deceived.*
- *Do not give up.*
- *Do not fight and argue.*
- *Do not be prideful.*
- *Do not be selfish.*[3]

These commands are hills on which we must be willing to die, because they offer the only thing truly worth fighting for: reconciliation with God and reconciliation with one another. Following them deserves our very best effort. They are mountains worthy of our suffering. We'll die for the sake of Jesus, love, selflessness, generosity, and grace.

Listen, I get it. The world is broken. Our country is a mess. There is much that needs fixing. Even so, the only thing that ultimately matters is reconciliation. And that hill worth dying on can only be found in no man's land.

The kings of Babylon dripped with ungodliness, yet Daniel served them well. But when King Darius outlawed prayer to God, Daniel's disobedience landed him in a lion's den. Daniel found his hill.

Joseph skillfully served the pagan Potiphar. Surely it troubled his conscience, yet he said yes to the Egyptian ruler. But when Potiphar's wife tried to seduce him, Joseph said no. The jealous wife concocted a story and threw him into prison. Joseph found his hill.

Esther won a beauty contest and became the queen of Persia, marrying the unsavory King Xerxes. She cooperated with the immoral traditions of the Persians. But when Mordecai told her of the plot to annihilate the Jews, she realized she was born "for such a time as this" (Esther 4:14). She risked her life to save her people. Esther found her hill.

Paul loved his Jewish brothers and pleaded with them to turn to Jesus. But when the Jewish leaders of cities threatened, beat, jailed, and even stoned him for preaching Christ's love for all people, Paul found his hill.

When you grow weary of trying to determine what hills are worth your death, remember Jesus Christ. Colossians 1:21 says we were once enemies with God. Too often we minimize our rebellion against God. We say things like "I was a bit adrift," or "I was a little out of step with God."

Stop it.

Admit it.

You betrayed him.

You chose to be his enemy.

You jumped in Satan's bunker.

Your rebellion magnifies the enormity of God's grace. Christ died for you, even though you were lobbing bombs at him and his plans. Your sins warranted death, but Jesus took your place. At Calvary, Jesus found his hill.

And we are called to do the same. In the midst of a world of bunkers, we are called to jump into the middle of the battlefield and stand for truth and peace. When we see the banner of Christ ascending over the flags of this world, when we see the potential of families forgiving, neighbors reconciling, and hearts changing, we'll know we've found our hill. On that hill, we're willing to suffer and die so that others may live.

HOPE

I cling to the story of Peter, because it gives me hope for the bunkered. I've told you bits of his "bunker" story, but let me summarize it.

God kept trying to teach Peter to welcome Gentiles to Jesus: Jesus taught him and showed him, the Holy Spirit stirred countless conversions in Gentile communities, and God sent Peter a vision followed by a miraculous encounter with Cornelius. Even after all of this, Peter fell back into his old, prejudiced, hurtful ways, so Paul confronted him and set him straight (Galatians 2). That's a lot of effort to get one guy out of his bunker, but oh, was it ever worth it.

When I begin to lose patience with someone stuck in a bunker, I remember Peter. Since God showed grace and patience with him, we will show grace and patience with others. And I'll be forever thankful for the grace and patience God has shown to me.

God's grace then overflows to others. Do you remember the first part of the story of Esau and Jacob? After Jacob deceived his father and wronged his twin brother, Esau, he fled. The two remained separated for more than twenty years. While away, Jacob got his own taste of deception's bitter pill. His own father-in-law tricked him into marrying *the other daughter* (which is a story for another day).

When Jacob obeyed God and packed his family to go meet Esau, he prepared for the worst. Four hundred men marched with Esau, while fear gripped Jacob. Jacob split his family into two groups, so that if Esau attacked, one of the groups might have a chance of escape. To Jacob's surprise and delight, the reunion went better than expected: "Esau ran to meet Jacob and embraced him; he threw his arms around his neck and kissed him. And they wept."[4] The impossible happened. The brothers reconciled.

Esau saw Jacob's family, no doubt watching the spectacle with great curiosity, and asked for an introduction. Jacob obliged, and we learn that the last child to be introduced was Joseph. Yes, *that* Joseph. This is the same Joseph who was sold into slavery by his brothers. This is the same Joseph who, after ascending to the second highest position in all of Egypt, forgave his brothers. The reconciliation he saw between his father and uncle became the reconciliation he lived as a man.

If Jacob and Esau could climb out of their bunkers and be reconciled, you and your worst enemy can too. If Joseph could forgive his brothers rather than exacting revenge, you can too. God can turn revenge into forgiveness, hate into love, deception into trust, enemies into brothers. He can rewrite the future of your family tree. He's done it before, and he will do it again. Don't give up hope. Ever.

THE RESTORATION

Humankind's unity with God was shattered in a garden—the Garden of Eden.[5] Sin divided humans from God. Adam and Eve's relationship also suffered wounds. Adam blamed Eve for his sin. I imagine as they trudged out of the Garden, Eve cursed, "Thanks a lot for throwing me under the bus, dude!" Sin fractures our relationship with God and our relationships with each other.

It only took two generations for us to start killing each other. Cain, Adam and Eve's oldest son, grew jealous of Abel, his younger brother.[6] The difference in their gifts to God revealed the differences in their hearts. Thus, God was more pleased with Abel. Instead of repenting, Cain pouted and let contempt give birth to murder. Cain killed his own brother.

When God asked Cain where Abel was, Cain protested, "Am I my brother's keeper?" He operated on the false premise that God doesn't demand we look after each other. God responded, "Do you not hear his blood crying out from the ground?"

Are you listening? You are your brother's keeper. And your sister's, cousin's, friend's, neighbor's, and stranger's.

The sin in the Garden bared its ugly teeth. It still does. But what was shattered in a garden will be restored in a city.

The bunkers around you may make you disillusioned, but the picture John painted in Revelation points us toward joy. John saw a vision of things to come: a new earth and a new city, Jerusalem, descending. Its eternal residents will live with no more pain, hardship, or sorrow. The lion will lie down with the lamb. Peace will reign.

> After this I looked, and there before me was a great multitude
> that no one could count, from every nation, tribe, people
> and language, standing before the throne and before the
> Lamb. They were wearing white robes and were holding
> palm branches in their hands. And they cried out in a
> loud voice:
>
> "Salvation belongs to our God,
> who sits on the throne,
> and to the Lamb."[7]

The massive crowd is diverse, loud, and spectacular. Yet their attention is not on themselves; it's on Jesus. They're singing the same song. "Salvation belongs to God." You and I stand on level ground when our eyes are on Christ. So let's turn our eyes away from our wants and others' shortcomings. Let's look to our only hope to exit our bunkers and take the path toward freedom: the path to reconciliation with God and each other. Let's pray. Let's lace up our work boots. Let's walk together. And when we find our hill on which to die, we'll find our hill on which to dance.

REFLECTION QUESTIONS

1. What have you learned to identify as a "bunker"?

2. What molehills have you treated as mountains?

3. What will you be doing differently since reading this book?

4. Would you commit to reading Revelation 7:9 every day this week?

5. Spend some quiet time praying about your journey from bunkers to no man's land to freedom.

LEAD YOUR FAMILY
12 READY-TO-USE STEPS FOR
SPIRITUALLY LEADING YOUR FAMILY

BRIAN JENNINGS
FOREWORD BY KYLE IDLEMAN

NOTES

CHAPTER 1: ROOTS

1. *The Free Dictionary*, s.v. "bunker mentality," accessed November 30, 2017, https://www.thefreedictionary.com/bunker+mentality.
2. First Christian Church of Chicago is an ethnically diverse church committed to changing its South Chicago neighborhood. By The Hand Club for Kids now has four Chicago locations helping over one thousand of the most at-risk youth in Chicago find abundant life. I love both places deeply. See http://www.firstchristianchicago.org; http://bythehand.org.
3. Due to the pushback, officials changed their minds and kept Manierre open. For an insightful article, see http://www.dnainfo.com/chicago/20130322/old-town/cps-school-closings-put-focus-on-gang-territories-neighborhoods.
4. 2 Chronicles 10.
5. Dr. Timothy Keller, "Preaching to the Heart" (lecture, 2014 John Reed Miller Lectures on Preaching, Jackson Reformed Theological Seminary, Jackson, MS, November 11–13, 2014).

CHAPTER 2: SPIRITUAL THREAT

1. Stephen Rex Brown, "Coal All Around! South Carolina Family Nearly Comes to Blows over Christmas Tree: Cops," *New York Daily News*, December 11, 2013, http://www.nydailynews.com/news/national/south-carolina-family-blows-christmas-tree-cops-article-1.1544389#commentpostform.
2. Doesn't this line sound like the start of a great book or movie? Hollywood, we need another bucket movie!
3. "Beyond the Pail—The Unbelievable War for the Oaken Bucket," Military History Now, June 26, 2012, http://militaryhistorynow.com/2012/06/26/beyond-the-pail-the-unbelievable-war-for-the-oaken-bucket/. See also *Wikipedia*, s.v. "War of the Bucket," last modified November 8, 2017, 2:58, http://en.wikipedia.org/wiki/War_of_the_Bucket.

4. Love, joy, peace, forbearance, kindness, goodness, faithfulness, gentleness, and self-control.
5. Kenny Boles, s.v. "factions," https://occ.edu/events/words. (You can find other helpful Greek word studies from Boles at this site too.)
6. See 1 Corinthians 5.
7. Luke 7:47.

CHAPTER 3: COLLATERAL DAMAGE
1. Genesis 25:19-34.
2. Genesis 37:1-4.
3. Mark 9:42.
4. Please read more about Blackbox at blackboxinternational.org.
5. 1 Timothy 4:12.
6. 1 Peter 2:12 (MSG).

CHAPTER 4: FRIEND OR FOE
1. Général Alexandre Percin, *Le Massacre de Notre Infanterie 1914–1918* (Paris: Michel Albin, 1921). Percin supported his claims using hundreds of items of correspondence from officers and men who had served in the French army in WWI.
2. Matthew 6:21.
3. Sun Tzu, *The Art of War*, trans. Lionel Giles (CreateSpace, 2016), 9.
4. Richard Furman, "Exposition of the Views of the Baptists Relative to the Coloured Population . . . ," The Gilder Lehrman Center for the Study of Slavery, Resistance, and Abolition, accessed November 30, 2017, https://glc.yale.edu /exposition-views-baptists-relative-coloured-population.
5. Richard Furman, "Exposition of the Views of Baptists Relative to the Coloured Population in the United States in a Communication to the Governor of South Carolina," 2nd ed. (Charleston: A. E. Miller, 1838), 6.
6. While this topic deserves more than a note, I must address a tragic mistake that is often made. People are saying, "Because some misused the Bible to defend slavery, we can never trust our own interpretation." This is foolish. A helpful question is "Did the slavery-defending preachers correctly interpret Scripture?" And a wise person concludes, "Because many have misused and misinterpreted Scripture, we must be more cautious, humble, and studious when reading, even if it means we come away 'undecided' on certain issues." Abraham Lincoln offered a constructive perspective on religious warfare. "My concern is not whether God is on our side; my greatest concern is to be on God's side" (Rev. Matthew Simpson attributed this quote to Lincoln in his address delivered at Lincoln's funeral).
7. Ephesians 6 explains who our battle is *not* against and who it *is* against, and also describes the weapons we have.
8. John 13:35.

CHAPTER 5: ARE YOU IN A BUNKER?
1. I have no clue about Clooney's political leanings. I thought about looking it up, but instead chose to watch *O Brother, Where Art Thou?* in ignorant bliss.
2. John Piper, *Bloodlines: Race, Cross, and the Christian* (Wheaton, IL: Crossway, 2011).

CHAPTER 6: DAUNTING AND INVITING

1. The movie *Warhorse* depicts this well.
2. I have listened to the sermon Hill preached at his wife's funeral more than any other in my life. See http://www.youtube.com/watch?v=T-WZyV6LMK0.

CHAPTER 7: GRACE AND TRUTH

1. Dr. Henry Cloud, *Changes That Heal: How to Understand Your Past to Ensure a Healthier Future* (Grand Rapids, MI: Zondervan, 1993), 23.
2. Dr. James Emery White, "Grace and Truth," Crosswalk.com (blog), October 8, 2012, http://www.crosswalk.com/blogs/dr-james-emery-white/grace-and-truth.html.
3. John 14:6.
4. Dietrich Bonhoeffer and Gerhard Leibholz, *The Cost of Discipleship* (New York: Macmillan, 1958).
5. Randy Alcorn summarizes his book *The Grace and Truth Paradox* with this quote, which can be read here: http://www.epm.org/resources/2010/Mar/13/grace-and -truth-paradox-responding-christlike-bala/ (accessed November 30, 2017).
6. Caleb Kaltenbach, *Messy Grace* (Colorado Springs: WaterBrook Press, 2015). See http://messygracebook.com.
7. Shane L. Windmeyer, "Dan and Me: My Coming Out as a Friend of Dan Cathy and Chick-fil-A," *HuffPost* (blog), January 28, 2013, http://www.huffingtonpost .com/shane-l-windmeyer/dan-cathy-chick-fil-a_b_2564379.html.

CHAPTER 8: WISDOM AND TACT

1. My missionary friends in countries where the gospel cannot be openly preached see God continue to influence people through dreams. Many cultures understand dreams to be direct communications from God, not the result of bad pizza.
2. Daniel 2:5.
3. Daniel 2:9.
4. Dictionary.com, s.v. "tact," accessed November 30, 2017, http://www.dictionary .com/browse/tact.
5. Daniel 1:5-14 implies that Daniel asked, "Will you agree to this experiment/challenge?" Daniel also asks a question to Arioch in Daniel 2:15 and to the king in Daniel 2:16.
6. Daniel's three friends were named Hananiah, Mishael, and Azariah. Nebuchadnezzar assigned them new names, which I'll use for the sake of familiarity.
7. God did choose to save them. See Daniel 3, especially Daniel 3:18.
8. See Daniel 6.
9. I respect this general policy. It's not ideal to adopt a child while preparing to birth one too. That's a lot to ask of parents.
10. My paraphrase; see Daniel 2:27-35.
11. My paraphrase; see Daniel 2:37-45.
12. For a great example with many parallels, see the story of Joseph, who served Pharaoh.
13. Matthew 22:21. More about this statement later.
14. Nate Boyer, "Ex-Green Beret Nate Boyer Writes Open Letter to Trump, Kaepernick, NFL and America," *ESPN*, October 13, 2017, http://www.espn.com/nfl/story/_/id /21003968/nfl-2017-ex-green-beret-nate-boyer-writes-open-letter-president-donald -trump-colin-kaepernick-nfl-united-states-america.

CHAPTER 9: GENTLENESS AND STRENGTH

1. Plato, *Plato's Republic*, trans. G. M. A. Grube, rev. C. D. C. Reeve (Indianapolis: Hackett, 1992), 166.
2. Moses (Numbers 12:3, AMP); Jesus (Matthew 11:29; 2 Corinthians 10:1).
3. John 11:35.
4. 1 Timothy 4:8.

CHAPTER 10: CONVICTION AND DISCERNMENT

1. Mark 12:13-15.
2. Ethelbert Stauffer, *Christ and the Caesars* (Philadelphia: Westminster Press, 1955).
3. At one point, enough resistance was mounted that Pilate lost the right to make coins. The British Museum even has a coin that was overprinted with a less-offensive message. Stauffer, *Christ and the Caesars*, 119.
4. Raymond Brown, *An Adult Christ at Christmas: Essays on the Three Biblical Christmas Stories, Matthew 2 and Luke 2* (Collegeville, MN: Liturgical Press, 1978). Also see Acts 5:36-38.
5. "Vintage Church - Jesus Video #3," YouTube video, 2:22, posted by "Vintage Church," March 10, 2008, http://www.youtube.com/watch?v=pCTAgxsLE3Q.
6. "Miss Sarajevo," recorded live in Milan in 2005, compact disc, track 8 of disc 2 on U2, *U218 Singles (Deluxe Version)*, Interscope, 2006.
7. Matthew 22:21. "Give back" is an accurate translation of "give." Jesus prods us to ask, "To whom does it belong?"
8. Matthew 17:24-27.

CHAPTER 11: SHREWDNESS AND INNOCENCE

1. Acts 16:16-40.
2. Acts 7.
3. See three examples in Luke 20. "And no one dared to ask him any more questions" (Luke 20:40).
4. I'm certain Randy Gariss wouldn't mind an epitaph that read "He preached too much about evangelism."
5. Flavius Josephus, *Antiquities of the Jews—Book III*, chap. 8, http://penelope .uchicago.edu/josephus/ant-3.html.
6. Scholars suspect that the perfume was nard, which was extremely pricey.
7. Mark 5:21-43.

CHAPTER 12: HUMILITY AND COURAGE

1. Erwin Raphael McManus, *Uprising: A Revolution of the Soul* (Nashville: Thomas Nelson, 2003), 101.
2. Ben, I apologized, but I never really felt like you believed me. Perhaps the ice and swelling around your ear prevented you from hearing my sincere attempt. So, anyway, I'm sorry you were wounded from my impressive throw.
3. "42 Trailer 2 (HD) (English & French Subtitles)," *42*, YouTube video, 2:33, posted by "Subtitled Trailers," January 11, 2013, https://www.youtube.com /watch?v=WjLPCypWzmw.
4. Charles Johnson, *Dreamer: A Novel* (New York: Scribner, 1999), 139.

CHAPTER 13: THE WAY THROUGH

1. Ray Sarlin, "One Step from My Grave!," 1st Battalion 50th Infantry Association, accessed November 20, 2017, http://www.ichiban1.org/html/stories/story_49.htm.

2. I found accounts of Ingo's story at John Dyson, "Escape from East Germany," *Reader's Digest Canada*, January 2010, http://www.readersdigest.ca/features/heart /escape-east-germany/ and "Germany: Escaping the East by Any Means," *Al Jazeera*, November 12, 2009, http://www.aljazeera.com/focus/2009/10/200910793416112 389.html.

3. Ta-Nehisi Coates, *Between the World and Me* (New York: Spiegel & Grau, 2015). Even though I was saddened by his hopeless despair, it's still a book from which I learned. I listened to the audio version, which was incredible. His poetic style of writing, combined with excellent speaking, really is genius.

CHAPTER 14: DIVIDED DIVERSITY

1. David von Drehle, Jay Newton-Small, and Maya Rhodan, "How Do You Forgive a Murder?," *Time*, November 23, 2015, http://time.com/time-magazine-charleston -shooting-cover-story/.

2. I strongly recommend reading anything written by John Perkins. I'd start with his autobiography, *Let Justice Roll Down* (Grand Rapids, MI: Baker Books, 2014). John M. Perkins is cofounder of the Christian Community Development Association and director of the John M. Perkins Foundation for Reconciliation and Development in Jackson, Mississippi. He is the author of many books, including *Let Justice Roll Down*.

3. Christian Community Development Association (website), accessed November 21, 2017, http://www.ccda.org.

4. Dr. John Perkins, in discussion with the author, June 24, 2015.

5. Dr. John Perkins, in discussion with the author, June 24, 2015.

6. Anne Lamott, *Bird by Bird: Some Instructions on Writing and Life* (New York: Anchor, 1995), 22. Lamott attributes this saying to "my priest friend Tom."

7. Martin Luther King Jr., sermon, "How Should a Christian View Communism?," 1963, accessed November 30, 2017, http://insidethecoldwar.org/sites/default/files /documents/How%20Should%20A%20Christian%20View%20Communism _0.pdf.

8. John Piper, *Bloodlines: Race, Cross, and the Christian* (Wheaton, IL: Crossway, 2011), 91.

9. Do you doubt this? Please read Mark DeYmaz, *Building a Healthy Multi-ethnic Church: Mandate, Commitments and Practices of a Diverse Congregation* (Hoboken, NJ: Jossey-Bass, 2007).

10. Galatians 3:28.

11. Nate Pyle (@NatePyle79), "To understand racism you need to understand power dynamics," Twitter, October 17, 2017, 3:12 p.m., https://twitter.com/natepyle79 /status/920412340922798080?lang=en.

12. Summary of a Facebook post by my friend Steve Chapman, who serves at First Christian Church, a multiethnic church on Chicago's South Side. Used with permission. Steve Chapman, "At her best, the church led the way in the development of social views about race," Facebook, https://www.facebook.com /steven.chapman.7796?fref=ts.

13. Read about some of the steps Highland Park Christian Church has taken here: http://www.dreamofdestiny.com/highland-park-cc-a-multi-ethnic-ministry-spotlight/.

14. Recommended reading for those wanting to dive deeper into understanding diversity and promoting reconciliation:

Mark DeYmaz, *Building a Healthy Multi-ethnic Church: Mandate, Commitments and Practices of a Diverse Congregation* (Hoboken, NJ: Jossey-Bass, 2007).

Edward Gilbreath, *Reconciliation Blues: A Black Evangelical's Inside View of White Christianity* (Downers Grove, IL: IVP Books, 2006).

Tony Evans, *Kingdom Man: Every Man's Destiny, Every Woman's Dream* (Carol Stream, IL: Focus on the Family, 2012).

Benjamin Watson, *Under Our Skin: Getting Real about Race. Getting Free from the Fears and Frustrations that Divide Us* (Carol Stream, IL: Tyndale, 2016). (This is the first book I recommend to fellow Christians just starting on this path.)

John M. Perkins, *Let Justice Roll Down* (Grand Rapids, MI: Baker, 2014). (Named by *Christianity Today* as one of the top fifty books that have shaped evangelicals; see http://www.christianitytoday.com/ct/2006/october/23.51.html.)

Ronald Takaki, *A Different Mirror: A History of Multicultural America* (New York: Little, Brown & Company, 1993). (Helpful for those who've never considered the plight of minority groups in America.)

Harriet Beecher Stowe, *Uncle Tom's Cabin; or, Life Among the Lowly* (New York: Penguin, 1986). (It changed the hearts of millions. It might change yours, too.)

Ephesians (all six chapters).

15. Edward Gilbreath, *Reconciliation Blues: A Black Evangelical's Inside View of White Christianity* (Downers Grove, IL: IVP Books, 2006), 178.

16. Gilbreath, *Reconciliation Blues*, 184–86.

17. Revelation 5:9; 7:9; 11:9; 13:7; 14:6.

CHAPTER 15: POLITICAL MAYHEM

1. Tony Evans, *Kingdom Man: Every Man's Destiny, Every Woman's Dream* (Carol Stream, IL: Focus on the Family, 2012), 8–9.

2. Edward Gilbreath, *Reconciliation Blues: A Black Evangelical's Inside View of White Christianity* (Downers Grove, IL: IVP Books, 2006), 133.

3. Amy E. Black and Stanley N. Gundry, eds., *Five Views on the Church and Politics* (Grand Rapids, MI: Zondervan, 2015). For an excellent summary, listen to the *Not So Black and White* podcast entitled "Five Views on Christianity and Politics" (Episode 18): https://itunes.apple.com/us/podcast/not-so-black-white-sean-palmer/id1121461268?mt=2.

4. Ethelbert Stauffer, *Christ and the Caesars* (Eugene, OR: Wipf and Stock Publishers, 2008), 149.

5. Tacitus, quoted in Frederick Widdowson, *A Bible Believer Looks at World History* (self-pub., Lulu.com, 2010), 124.

6. Mark Altrogge, "What It Means and Does Not Mean to Honor Our President," Bible Study Tools, accessed November 30, 2017, http://www.biblestudytools.com/blogs/mark-altrogge/what-it-means-and-does-not-mean-to-honor-our-president.html.

7. Dr. John Perkins, in discussion with the author, June 24, 2015.

8. Dick Alexander posted this on his Facebook page and granted me permission to use it. Dick Alexander, "A thought about a Christian's role in/with politics and government," Facebook, October 9, 2016, https://www.facebook.com/dick.alexander.758.

CHAPTER 16: CLASS WARFARE

1. From the Greek word *prosopolempsia*, which translates as "face-taking." See Kenny Boles, s.v. "partiality," https://occ.edu/events/words.
2. Acts 10:34.
3. For the sake of clarity, know that when I write *poor*, I'm speaking in economic terms. I understand the term can mean much more.
4. I heard James Whitford speak on this at the True Charity Initiative on April 22, 2015, in Tulsa, OK. He leads Watered Garden Ministry in Joplin, MO. I highly respect his wisdom and ministry.
5. Chris Horst, "The Challenge of Helping—Part 2," *Hope International* (blog), Hope International, March 30, 2009, http://blog.hopeinternational.org/2009/03/30/the-challenge-of-helping-part-2. Peter Greer, HOPE's president and CEO, heard this story while living in Rwanda right out of college (he tells the story in this video as well: https://vimeo.com/154617188). Permission granted by Sarah Ann Schultz, marketing communications specialist, HOPE.
6. Let me recommend four resources for those wanting to be wise in helping the poor: Steve Corbett and Brian Fikkert, *When Helping Hurts: How to Alleviate Poverty without Hurting the Poor . . . and Yourself*; Robert D. Lupton, *Toxic Charity: How Churches and Charities Hurt Those They Help (And How to Reverse It)*; Community Development Association (https://ccda.org/about/); and Alexis de Tocqueville, *Memoir on Pauperism* (http://www.civitas.org.uk/pdf/Tocqueville_rr2.pdf).
7. See also Proverbs 6:10-11; 10:4-5; 13:11-18; 20:4; 20:13; 21:5-6; 21:17-26; 22:13; 2 Thessalonians 3:10.
8. 2 Corinthians 8:9.
9. Greg Nettle and Santiago "Jimmy" Mellado, *Small Matters: How Churches and Parents Can Raise Up World-Changing Children* (Grand Rapids, MI: Zondervan, 2016).

CHAPTER 18: FAITH FIGHTS

1. Enid and Austin Bhebe, "We're Marching to Zion," Austinbhebe.com (blog), January 7, 2013, https://austinbhebe.wordpress.com/2013/01/07/were-marching-to-zion/.
2. Scot McKnight, *The Blue Parakeet: Rethinking How You Read the Bible* (Grand Rapids, MI: Zondervan, 2010), 23.
3. John 15:1-17.
4. John 17:20-26.
5. Romans 14.
6. Smith was the first to preach at a New Year's Day, 1832, unity meeting. The Restoration Movement garnered loose connections without denominational creeds or authorities. Like any movement, it had its high and low points. I believe the desire to discern between the big and little for the sake of unity was one of its most

helpful contributions. To read more, see http://www.therestorationmovement.com /index.htm.

7. I heard Chan tell this story live. You can find many of his excellent sermons here: http://www.sermonaudio.com/search.asp?speakeronly=true&currsection=sermons speaker&keyword=Francis+Chan.

8. Randy Gariss provided this advice during a phone conversation.

9. Acts 18.

10. Three thousand people were baptized in Acts 2, the Ethiopian in Acts 8, Paul in Acts 9, Cornelius in Acts 10, Lydia and a jailer in Acts 16. In Acts, when people chose to follow Christ, they believed, confessed, and repented, and they were baptized and renewed, which means forgiven of sins, given the gift of the Holy Spirit, born again, made new—the things only God can do in us. The New Testament writers use these five terms, but never at the expense of another (to say they were baptized doesn't negate the necessity of belief). So we should avoid dogmatism with any of the five. It's God who saves. Apollos's misunderstanding came because he knew about John's baptism, but he had not yet heard of baptism in Jesus' name (note Acts 18:23-25).

EPILOGUE: A HILL ON WHICH TO DIE

1. Quoted from Frederick Douglass's "West India Emancipation" speech, which was given at Canandaigua, NY, on August 3, 1857. See "(1857) Frederick Douglass, 'If There Is No Struggle, There Is No Progress,'" BlackPast.org, accessed November 30, 2017, http://www.blackpast.org/1857-frederick-douglass-if-there-no-struggle-there -no-progress.

2. Révérien Rurangwa, *Genocide: My Stolen Rwanda* (London: Reportage Press, 2009), quoted in Cat Knarr, "Remembering Rwanda on Good Friday," *HuffPost* (blog), April 6, 2012, https://www.huffingtonpost.com/catherine-newhouse /remembering-rwanda-on-good-friday_b_1403231.html.

3. Galatians 6:7; Hebrews 10:36; Proverbs 17:14; Proverbs 16:18; Philippians 2:3.

4. Genesis 33:4.

5. Genesis 3.

6. Genesis 4.

7. Revelation 7:9-10.

THE NAVIGATORS® STORY

THANK YOU for picking up this NavPress book! I hope it has
been a blessing to you.

NavPress is a ministry of The Navigators. The Navigators began
in the 1930s, when a young California lumberyard worker named
Dawson Trotman was impacted by basic discipleship principles and
felt called to teach those principles to others. He saw this mission as
an echo of 2 Timothy 2:2: "And the things you have heard me say in
the presence of many witnesses entrust to reliable people who will
also be qualified to teach others" (NIV).

In 1933, Trotman and his friends began discipling members of the
US Navy. By the end of World War II, thousands of men on ships
and bases around the world were learning the principles of spiritual
multiplication by the person-to-person teaching of God's Word.

After World War II, The Navigators expanded its ministry to include
college campuses; local churches; the Glen Eyrie Conference Center
and Eagle Lake Camps in Colorado Springs, Colorado; and neighborhood and citywide initiatives across the country and around the world.

Today, with more than 2,600 US staff members—and local ministries in more than 100 countries—The Navigators continue the process of making disciples who make more disciples, advancing the Kingdom of God in a world that desperately needs the hope and salvation of Jesus Christ and the encouragement to grow deeper in relationship with Him.

NAVPRESS was created in 1975 to advance the calling of The Navigators by bringing biblically rooted and culturally relevant products to people who want to know and love Christ more deeply. In January 2014, NavPress entered into an alliance with Tyndale House Publishers to strengthen and better position our rich content for the future. Through *The Message* Bible and other resources, NavPress seeks to bring positive spiritual movement to people's lives.

If you're interested in learning more or becoming involved with The Navigators, go to www.navigators.org. For more discipleship content from The Navigators and NavPress authors, visit www.thedisciplemaker.org. May God bless you in your walk with Him!

Sincerely,

DON PAPE
VP/PUBLISHER, NAVPRESS

www.navpress.com

CP1308